THE YEAR AHEAD

New beginnings

On a cool March morning, amber light filters through an intricate web of dark branches, where fresh buds begin to appear and new leaves start to unfurl. The next few months will see a drastic change as spring moves on and nature abounds. The presence of frolicking lambs in the fields becomes a welcome sight, often signalling the end of a long winter. As the clocks move forward one hour at the close of the month, the days are filled with light and warmth starts to stir the countryside. Mother Nature fills us with excitement and expectations of what the new season might bring.

Garden jobs

Simple steps to keep your plot
looking good this season

FLORAL GREETINGS

Bring some spring joy to your doorstep
by packing a container with colourful
spring plants. Primulas are the perfect
March pick-me-up and there are varieties
to suit all styles. New varieties in all sorts
of cheerful shades have recently come
onto the market, so browse online and be
prepared to fall in love.

GET WEEDING
As the soil starts to warm
up and days get longer,
weeds will thrive. Keep
on top of them before
they have a chance to set
seed and spread.

MULCH BEDS AND POTS

Add a layer of compost or leaf mould to add nutrients, smother weeds and keep in moisture. For pots, scrape away the top 2.5-5cm of compost and replace with John Innes No.3 (£4.87/35L, diy.com)

CARE FOR HOUSEPLANTS

Start watering and feeding your houseplants this month after their winter rest.

SORT OUT PATCHY LAWNS

Help your lawn bounce back after winter wear and tear by using a feed and seed product such as Patch Magic from Miracle-Gro (£15/1.5kg, wickes.co.uk). Pretty soon the patches will be filled in and your dream lawn will be back.

GROW SUNFLOWERS

Annual sunflowers are hard to beat for a shot of summer colour. Dwarf ones are perfect for the front of borders and pots, mid-height ones look good mixed in with other blooms in a bed and taller varieties are great for the back of borders. For long-lasting colour, try multi-branching 'Soleil' (£3.99/12 seeds, marshallsgarden.com).

PEP UP PATHS

Now's the time to replace rotten log rolls or loose mortar holding stone or brick edging, while plants aren't in the way. Add a fresh covering to gravel or chipped bark paths to give them a crisp finish too.

COVER A DULL FENCE

Plant wall shrub Chaenomeles superba 'Crimson and Gold' (£12.99/9cm pot, thompson-morgan.com) into moist but well-drained soil in full sun or dappled shade for vibrant red blooms in March and April.

DEADHEAD DAFFS

Remove fading flowers on daffodils to prevent seedpods forming, which saps the bulbs of energy. Leave the foliage to die down naturally.

FILL GAPS WITH COLOUR

Every bed needs some little gems to fill in the gaps at the front and spill over the edges. Alpine plants fit the bill nicely, and they're in garden centres at the moment. Try the alpine perennial collection of 30 plants for £22.47 from jparkers.co.uk.

Give summer bulbs a flying start– plant summer-flowering bulbs in pots in a greenhouse or conservatory so they can grow strong roots and shoots before going outside. Pop them in John Innes No.3 compost, then once any danger of frost has passed, take them outside for short amounts of time each day for around a week to get them used to being outdoors.

Wonderful wildlife

When it comes to nature, you might be surprised at the miraculous creatures living right on your doorstep

We are a nation of animal lovers, which seems especially true when you think about our numerous nature reserves. In seemingly unremarkable grassy fields or alongside rivers, efforts are underway to protect our rare and unique wildlife — from ospreys to cranes, red squirrels and puffins. Support them with a visit this spring.

WATERY WONDERS

Situated in Britain's smallest county, Rutland Water packs a punch when it comes to charming walks. It's one of the country's largest man-made lakes, and has its own 1,000-acre nature reserve with four miles of walking trails at its western end, maintained by the Leicestershire and Rutland Wildlife Trust.

One of the reserve's biggest success stories is that, around 20 years ago, it became home to the first pair of osprey to breed in Britain for 150 years, and the Rutland Osprey Project continues today, with hides to see them for yourself. Spring is also a good time to see great crested grebes, warblers, red kite, bluebells and common spotted orchids. Look out online for regular guided wildlife walks too, which cost £10pp.
■ For more information visit lrwt.org. uk/rutland-water

LORD OF THE DANCE

When black grouse want to impress a lady, they go all out! And spring is the perfect time to see them performing in 'leks' (another word for courtship rituals). This is just one of the seasonal delights on offer at the RSPB's enormous Inversnaid reserve, in Stirling, where you might also see pine martins, wood warblers, golden eagles, peregrines, osprey or perhaps the very endangered twite (a type of finch). There are trails of varying lengths to choose between and on the woodland and upland trails you can also look out for the remains of 17th and 18th Century buildings. Wherever you walk, arrive early enough for the dawn chorus and you'll have a truly humbling experience.
■ For more information visit rspb.org.uk

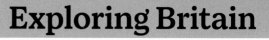

Exploring Britain

Spring

PARADISE ISLAND

For a day out that feels very exclusive, schedule a trip to Skomer Island. It might be less than a mile off the Pembrokeshire coast, but it's only open to visitors from April – October, and visits need to be booked in advance. A circular 3.7-mile walk will take you around the cliff edges, where you can hunt for puffins, Manx shearwaters, razorbills, gannets, grey seals, harbour porpoises, dolphins and fulmars. And that's without mentioning the island's stunning bluebell displays! As well as day trips you can also arrange to stay overnight on the island, in self-catering accommodation.

■ **For more information visit the Wildlife Trust of South and West Wales' website welshwildlife.org. Boat trips to Skomer cost £40 per adult, £30 for children aged 2 -12. To book, call 01646 603123 or visit Pembrokeshire-islands.co.uk**

CRANE YOUR NECK

When it comes to rare and endangered native species, Pensthorpe Natural Park in Norfolk shouldn't be overlooked. The 600-acre reserve is located both sides of the River Wensum, and is a safe haven for species including red squirrels, turtle doves and even majestic Eurasian cranes. The Pensthorpe Conservation Trust is at the forefront of efforts to protect these charismatic creatures, rearing captive bred corncrakes for release, exploring release sites for cranes, and undertaking bird ringing, wildlife monitoring and work to restore the river (which has been given special status as a site of scientific interest). There are numerous hides, walks and gardens to explore, as well as playgrounds for children to enjoy.

■ **Admission costs £9.95 adults, £8.95 children. For more information call 01328 851465 or visit pensthorpe.com**

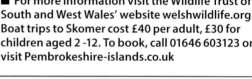

BIRDER'S PARADISE

Bird watching enthusiasts will be in heaven on a trip to Chapman's Well, Durham — it's considered one of the country's top spots, thanks to its abundance of feathered inhabitants. The landscape is a mixture of lowland heather, rich in heather, bilberry and juniper, combined with marshy grassland and abundant ponds. It's home to five species of owl, and other predatory birds including marsh harriers and red kites, as well as wading birds such as lapwings, curlew and redshanks. Meanwhile, Exmoor ponies are an important part of the conservation effort, as they munch away at the grass and allow space for wildflower meadows to develop.

■ **For more information visit durham.gov.uk**

Egg-stra special!

These punch needle napkins make the perfect decoration for your Easter table

You will need...

Washable pen or pencil
Punch needle set (available from Hobbycraft)
6in embroidery hoop
Assorted coloured embroidery floss

112cm x 2m (44 x 78in) white cotton fabric
Egg template
ALL MATERIALS AVAILABLE FROM HOBBYCRAFT.CO.UK

1 Take a photocopy of the template shown below, right.

2 Cut the fabric to your desired napkin size making sure to include 2cm seam allowance along each edge.

3 Using a window or light box place the template underneath the fabric and trace onto the fabric using a washable pen or pencil where you would like the embroidery to go. This will be the back of the fabric.

4 Secure the fabric in the embroidery hoop making sure the fabric is as tight as possible.

5 Select your first colour and thread your punch needle. Work around the edge of the first section. Once the edge is embroidered, continue to fill in the space, making sure to work in a brick layout and not in rows to avoid any gaps occurring. Try to keep your stitches consistent, approx 3mm apart.

6 Once one section is complete, change to the next colour you would like to use and again work around the edge and then continue to fill in the section.

7 Continue to change colour for each section, working the outline and then filling in each section until the egg is complete.

8 Tidy up the front of the work by cutting any longer threads.

9 Using a sewing machine, fold each side over, then over again to create a neat edge. Sew into place.

10 Cut any loose threads and lightly iron the napkin ready for use.

In full bloom

Lift your mood...

Touched by a warming sea breeze, drifts of billowing, cool-hued lavender ripple on slender stems above silvery leaves, like the ebb and flow of the tide. This intoxicating ocean of blue can be experienced by taking a trip to Norfolk Lavender – close to the county's north-west coast. Founded in 1932, this impressive lavender farm boasts nearly 100 aromatic acres of this plant that is so synonymous with summer. Lavender isn't the only treat that this season brings. The days are bright and fine, the shorter nights are cloaked in velvet stillness. Stepping out into a meadow filled with buttercups, and dandelions is an unalloyed delight. Even gentle showers of rain are welcomed as they quench the myriad of plants putting on a show with their leaves and flowers. The abundance of summer is everywhere – from the warm sun on your skin to the sweet sound of songbirds on the wind. Be sure to enjoy every moment.

Garden jobs

Simple steps to keep your plot looking good this season

FILL THAT GAP

Add instant colour to bare patches with summer bedding plants which you'll find aplenty in supermarkets and garden centres now. Big and blousy dahlias are a great choice. Their beautiful flowers come in almost every colour imaginable, from pale pastels to hot, vibrant shades. They come in a range of flower shapes, from small tight balls to lily-like blooms the size of dinner plates. They're perfect for adding late summer colour to borders from July to October and look good in any style of garden, from a cottage-style border to a jungle or exotic scheme. They look especially lovely with cosmos, grasses, Verbena bonariensis or cannas.

PAINT YOUR FENCE

Now the dry weather's here, give your fence a coat of paint for a colour boost and to protect against weathering. Scrub with soapy water first, leave to dry, then apply your chosen paint. We love Cuprinol 5 Year Ducksback (£14/5L, homebase.co.uk) as it's quick drying, low odour and safe to use around plants and pets, plus it won't break the bank if you need a few tins.

PROP UP BEARDED IRISES

Prevent wind-damaged stems by pushing a slim bamboo cane, the same height as the plant, into the soil and tying the stem to it loosely with twine.

GO POTTY FOR PELARGONIUMS

Garden centres will be full of these now so it's the perfect way to fill your garden with easy colour June-November. Pelargoniums shrug off heatwaves and won't keel over if you forget to water them for a day or two! Just pop them in a sunny spot and snip off dead flowers to keep them blooming.

CLEAN YOUR MOWER

Use a stiff brush to scrape away old grass and a softer one on more delicate areas. Wipe over with a damp cloth and then leave to dry before storing away.

PERK UP HOUSEPLANTS

Once the danger of frost has passed, move foliage plants outdoors for a little holiday in the sunshine. Put them in a spot where they'll get plenty of light but out of midday sun to prevent scorching, and water as normal.

EDGE YOUR LAWN

Do it every time you mow and it only takes a few minutes. A grass trimmer with a rotating head is the quickest and easiest way (try Powerbase 20V Cordless Grass Trimmer 25cm, £59, homebase.co.uk). If the trimmings are short, use a Dutch hoe to mix them into the soil where they will quickly rot down.

KEEP ROSES HEALTHY

Snip off faded flowers just above the leaf and feed with a rose fertiliser such as Toprose (£4.50/1kg, homebase.co.uk). Any tiny pear-shaped insects are aphids, and best dealt with by a squish between thumb and finger, or blast them with water.

TOP UP WATER FEATURES

Check regularly to make sure they don't run dry, which can damage the pump, and top up with fresh water. If done little and often, this helps to keep the water clear.

CONTROL IVY ON FENCES

If not trimmed back, the attractive, glossy, evergreen foliage can become a crowded mass that can damage the structure. Where ivy growth is thick, chop some back now, checking for birds' nests first.

CUT AND-COME-AGAIN SALADS

Snip little and often, preferably daily, and they will produce new leaves for longer. It's not too late to sow – add seeds (£2.25, chilternseeds.co.uk) to a large pot of multipurpose compost and water with one litre per 10-litre container.

CHOP SPRING BLOOMERS

Once perennials such as delphiniums, which provide early summer colour year after year, have finished blooming, cut back flower stems to just above the ground. This will encourage fresh foliage and, for some, a second flush of flowers later in summer. Add a handful of fertiliser such as Growmore (£6/4kg, wickes.co.uk) around the base.

Feel the wind in your hair and the waves lapping at your feet on a walk along one of the UK's coastal paths

There's nothing quite as evocative as staring out to sea on a summer's day, with the wind whipping at your clothes and the smell of salt spray in the air. Pack a picnic and explore some of our most picturesque coastlines to discover wildlife, historic architecture and strange natural phenomena.

Seaside strolls

WHISTLING SANDS

It sounds like something from a story, but 'Whistling Sands' is a real place, by Porthor on the north side of the Llŷn Peninsula.

As you might imagine, the beach is named for the distinctive noise made by the sand underfoot, and makes for an entertaining walk – not least because of the chance of spotting a seal or porpoise. Even if the animals aren't playing ball, you should be able to spot islands Dinas Bach and Dinas Fawr. The area's cliff slopes are being restored by the National Trust (which has a car park and toilet blocks available), while creatures including finches and yellowhammers are encouraged by a wildlife corridor.

■ Find more information at nationaltrust.org.uk/llyn-peninsula

A LOVELY LIGHTHOUSE

Souter, in Sunderland, is home to a gorgeous coastal path with plenty to see. It's reclaimed colliery land, that's now a wildlife haven thanks to its wetland habitats, ponds, and even an artificial sand martin nest bank.

For even better views, climb the 76 steps to the top of Souter Lighthouse (which couldn't look more traditional, thanks to its pretty red-and-white stripes) and you'll also discover how the lighthouse keeper used to live.

To the north is The Leas, two-and-a-half miles of limestone cliffs, which also makes for a nice stroll, and is the traditional finishing stretch for the famous Great North Run.

■ Find more information at nationaltrust.org.uk/souter-lighthouse-and-the-leas

Summer

JURASSIC JOY

Despite looking white and pure, the Old Harry Rocks in Dorset hide a murky past – they're thought to have been named after local pirate Harry Paye. Whatever other secrets they might hold, these chalk stacks make for dramatic photos and an intriguing way to explore the Jurassic Coast. Reach them on foot from Studland or Swanage, walking across chalk grassland with great views. Old Harry was once connected to The Needles on the Isle of Wight by a line of chalk hills that eroded away during the last Ice Age – on a clear day you can spot The Needles from Studland Bay. Spring and summer are particularly good times to visit, as you can spot rare pink pyramidal orchids here.
■ **For more information visit jurassiccoast.org**

LITERARY LINK

Pack your garlic when you take on the 4.5km Cruden Bay to the Bullers of Buchan route, in Aberdeenshire. Why? Because you'll go past the eerie ruins of Slains Castle, thought to have inspired Dracula, by Bram Stoker, who was once a guest there! You might also recognise it from The Crown, as the Queen Mother was seen there in series one. Originally built in 1579, it was abandoned in 1925, and the roof was removed to avoid taxation. Cruden Bay itself is an expanse of pink sands and dunes, beloved by day trippers and fishing enthusiasts alike.
■ **For more information visit walkhighlands.co.uk**

A BIRDER'S PARADISE

Explore the route between Whitehaven and St Bees, in Cumbria, and you might be lucky enough to spot a puffin! It's also home to black guillemots and terns. Other points of interest include St Bees lighthouse, and the monument marking the start of the Coast to Coast walk. There's the opportunity to drop down into various bays along the way, including Fleswick which has semi-precious stones hidden in its shingle It's a reasonably lengthy cliff top walk at 6.5 miles, but you can easily get the train back to Whitehaven at the end – after a cup of tea in the pretty red sandstone village of St Bees.
■ **For more information visit coasttocoast.uk**

Pretty & practical!

This home-sewn cutlery wrap is ideal for alfresco eating this summer

You will need....

Sewing machine
Dressmaking
scissors
Tape measure
Needles
Pins
White thread
Pack of flower print
fat quarters
(4 quarters in a pack)
Ultra thick batting
Ribbon

ALL MATERIALS AVAILABLE FROM
HOBBYCRAFT.CO.UK

1 Start by measuring your cutlery to get a guide of how big your cutlery roll needs to be. Measure out your fabrics and wadding. You could make these any size you would like however, for this example, you will need:

Fabric (4 pieces)
• 1 piece 28 x 28cm (11 x 11in) for the main outside (we have used a fabric print design with green roses).
• 1 piece 28 x 28cm (11 x 11in) for the main inside (we have used a plain contrasting grey fabric).
• 1 piece 17 x 28cm (6½ x 11in)
• 1 piece 22 x 28cm (8½ x 11in) for the inside cutlery holding parts (we have used a fabric print design with anemones). Press.

Wadding
2 pieces 28cm x 28cm (11 x 11in)

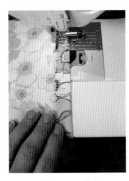

2 Take one of the inside cutlery-holding smaller pieces of fabric and fold over by a 1cm (½in) seam allowance. Using a straight running stitch, sew to secure this edge into place. Repeat with the other inside cutlery-holding piece.

3 Take one piece of wadding and lay your main inside piece of fabric on to this. On top of this, line up the inner cutlery pieces with the edges at the bottom and pin into position. You'll be sewing this one piece of wadding and all of these pieces of fabric together, straight down from the top of these two cutlery holder pieces, to the bottom of the cutlery roll every 7cm (2½ in) (3 times). Measure, and pin to mark where these will be.

4 Now sew from the top of these two cutlery holder pieces, to the bottom of the cutlery roll every 7cm (2 ½ in) as pinned or marked. Use the edges of the fabric as a guide for a straight line.

5 Cut your ribbon long enough to be over twice the width of your roll. For this example, we cut our ribbon to be 66cm (30in) long. This allows a little extra and some seam allowance. Fold in half.

6 Take your now sewn inside part and lay this down right sides up. On to this, in the middle, place your folded ribbon at the right-hand side edge. On top of this place and line up your outside piece of fabric right sides down. Finally, lay down and line up the other piece of wadding. You will now be sewing all these together into position, so pin into position if desired.

7 Starting from the bottom of the cutlery roll and using a 5mm (9¼ in) seam allowance, sew all the way around the edge leaving a gap for turning out. Secure your threads.

Trim your edges slightly to neaten and to remove any excess edges, snip the corners to help with turning out. Turn out through the gap and press if required.

8 Starting from the top of the cutlery holding part, sew in a straight-line stitch (or use a decorative stitch if preferred!), sew down to the bottom, pivot, sew along the bottom (to secure the gap closed) and back up to the top of the cutlery holding part. Secure your threads.

9 Add your cutlery inside and your roll is now complete! You could even use it to store crochet hooks.

Mists and mellow

fruitfulness

Autumn is a magical time of year, as we watch the vibrant greens of summer turn slowly but steadily into gold, ochres, oranges and reds. There is rich glow to the world, a feeling of abundance and vibrancy. Country lanes are bursting with shiny, rich fruits peeping through the hedgerows. Those who are brave enough to navigate the brambles and purple-stained fingers are rewarded with a bumper crop of blackberries. This is the season of crumbles, pies and jams; of warm cosy jumpers, log fires and woolly socks as Mother Nature takes us by the hand and gently leads us towards winter.

SHAPE UP LAVENDER

Trim using secateurs, taking off all the faded blooms by cutting back flower stems and around 2.5-5cm of the leafy growth below them.

Simple steps to keep your plot looking good this season

Garden jobs

GIVE BIRDS A TREAT

Make your own bird feeders. Cut the fruit in half and scoop out the flesh. Punch holes into the skin of each halve, using a metal skewer, then poke through some sticks. Fill with bird seed mix and hang from a tree with twine.

RECYCLE COMPOST

It's best not to reuse compost from pots of now-spent summer flowers as the plants will have taken up all the nutrients. But it's a great soil improver. Tip it out onto a bare patch in your border now, leave it to break down over winter, then dig it into the soil in spring.

GROW CURLY KALE

It's super-healthy, tastes delicious roasted with a little olive oil and sea salt, and makes a striking winter pot feature. Grow two plants in a 30cm-wide pot filled with multipurpose compost. Place in a sunny spot and water well in dry periods. Add any liquid fertiliser weekly once growing well.

EMBRACE EVERGREENS

As sun-drenched borders start to lose their sparkle, shade-loving evergreens will soon be having their garden moment. You'll find foliage in striking shapes and colours that'll look good all through winter. Polystichum setiferum 'Herrenhausen' is a lacy, low-growing soft shield fern that's easy to grow in any soil type.

POP BULBS IN POTS

Plant snowdrops now, available from garden centres, for a late-winter display. Grab a pot with drainage holes, part-fill with potting compost, push in bulbs so their final depth is at three times their length, top with compost and water. When shoots appear in January, move to a partially shaded spot to flower.

KEEP PONDWATER CLEAR

Cover your pond with a net to prevent leaves from falling into the water, making it murky and blocking up the filter. Secure in place with metal pegs or stones.

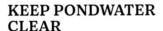

MAKE SOIL CONDITIONER

In a sheltered spot in your garden, fashion a bin from chicken wire. Throw in leaves and in a year's time you'll have your own leaf-mould soil conditioner to dig into flowerbeds.

ENJOY FRESH GARLIC

Along with onion, garlic is used in so many delicious recipes and it's easy to grow your own. It's best planted now, and we recommend the 'Elephant' variety (£8.50/3 cloves, sarahraven.com) for giant, juicy cloves that are perfect for roasting. Push the individual cloves into any compost to twice their own depth, pointy ends up, and about 15cm apart, and they'll be ready by June to crush into soup, stews, a stir-fry or whatever you fancy.

Forests of wonder

It's time to kick up the leaves, star gaze, and seek out woodland creatures before they snuggle down for winter

Wandering in woods is renowned for its physical and mental health benefits - but it's also a lovely way to spot wildlife, understand local history, or get to know a new part of the UK. Treat your inner Robin Hood with a visit to one of these fascinating woodland spaces.

FAIRYTALE FEELINGS

For a day out that Snow White would approve of, step into the magical Gwydir Forest Park, in Snowdonia. The landscape is a patchwork of lakes, forests and mountains, in the heart of the Snowdonia National Park. It feels as if the mossy tree roots and twisted climbing plants are filled with fairy magic, and it helps that the area is rich with myths and legends, such as those of Dafydd ap Siencyn, a Robin Hood-type of figure. There are various marked walking trails to follow, from a sedate boardwalk to hillier challenges.

■ For more information visit **visitsnowdonia.info/gwydir-forest-park**

STAR SPOTTING

Dalby Forest, Yorkshire, is recognised as one of the best places to see the night sky in England, and has been named a Dark Sky Discovery Site – there's a camping site that's perfect for would-be star-spotters. But it's not just for night owls – the 8,000 acres of woodland have 13 walking trails (as well as six for cyclists, with bike hire available), two play areas, an activity centre and a cafe. There's also a reason to come back in the future, as construction is currently underway on a dry stone wall maze.

■ Find trails and other information at **forestryengland.uk/dalby-forest**

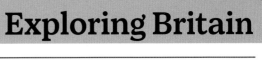

HISTORIC WILDERNESS

It may be called the 'New' Forest, but in fact the historic woodland dates back to the Domesday Book. This pretty area covers around 300 square miles, and of course its most famous attribute is the 5,000 resident wild ponies, who cover the forest roaming freely (and are given priority over cars). Consider staying in the pretty village of Brockenhurst, which has been ranked by estate agents as Britain's most beautiful place to live, and where ponies and deer are known to wander the streets. Challenge yourself with a seven-mile route to the neighbouring town of Lymington, which takes in woodlands and charming country paths, and reward yourself with a cream tea or meal out, before taking the train back.

■ **For ideas on where to stay in Brockenhurst, and lots of cycling routes, visit visitbrockenhurst.co.uk**

LOVELY LOCH

It's worth keeping your eyes peeled in the Loch Ard Forest (which runs from Aberfoyle to the hills beside Loch Lomond), as you never know what you might spot. For one thing, there's the loch itself to discover – it's ideal for wild swimming if you can brave the chill – and if you're lucky you might also see resident roe deer, red squirrels, otters, water voles or osprey. Even on a day when the wildlife won't play ball, there are animal sculptures by artist and environmentalist Rob Mulholland to look out for. There are plenty of routes to explore, including a four-and-a-half mile trail to take in the sculptures.

■ **Find walking trails and more information at forestryandland.gov.scot**

RE-GREENING THE MIDLANDS

The Midlands have historically been the site of heavy industry and coal mining, but there's an ambitious project to bring back their green woodlands. The National Forest project, started in 1995, covers 200 square miles across Derbyshire, Leicestershire and Staffordshire, and 80 per cent of it can be accessed by the public. There are numerous spots to visit, but why not start with Beacon Hill Country Park, Leicestershire — one of the area's highest spots, and the site of a Bronze Age hill fort. It's a mixture of woodland, grassland, wetlands and heath, and home to grazing alpaca! There are cycling, walking and all-abilities paths across the park.

■ **For information on Beacon Hill, visit leicscountryparks.org.uk. It's free but parking charges apply.**

■ **For more information on the National Forest project, visit nationalforest.org**

Make your own pretty autumn display with these easy-to-sew pumpkins

Home-sewn veg

You will need...

Sewing machine
Fabric scissors
Embroidery needles
Pins
White cotton thread
2x pack of Cotton Fat
Quarters (5 quarters
per pack) in shades of
yellow and orange
1 x pack of Hessian
natural Fat Quarters
Pack of decorative
cinnamon sticks
200g soft toy stuffing
Orange embroidery
thread

ALL MATERIALS AVAILABLE FROM
HOBBYCRAFT.CO.UK

1 Cut out a narrow semi-circle template as pictured, depending on the size of pumpkin you desire. Then, you'll need to cut out 8 shapes of the same size in your chosen fabric.

2 Place 2 of the fabric shapes right sides together and sew down one edge from top to bottom.
■ **Top tip:** In order to give added strength to your seam, make sure you backstitch a couple of stitches at the top and bottom otherwise the seam is more likely to become undone when stuffing your pumpkin.

3 Repeat this process for all 8 pieces, stitching each piece together and leaving a small gap in the final side seam to allow for turning.

4 Turn the pumpkin out the right way and remove any excess threads. Stuff the pumpkin firmly to shape and sew up the gap in the side seam.

5 Using three strands of embroidery thread and starting at the bottom of the pumpkin, wrap the thread around each side seam until all eight sides are covered, then gently pull the pumpkin into shape.

6 Add a stem to your pumpkin through the top opening – you could use a roll of burlap or hessian, felt, twigs or cinnamon sticks. Make a running stitch around the top opening and secure tightly. Add ribbons and leaves to accessorise your decoration. Your pumpkin is complete! Make as many as you want in the same way but experiment with different sizes and fabrics.

Winter's wonder

Beautiful Britain

On a cold winter's night, when temperatures have dropped below freezing, delicate fringes of crystalline frost coat the landscape; feathered fingers dust the grass in patterns of silver. As dawn approaches and the sky begins to brighten a generous dusting of white icing is slowly revealed. The beauty and delicacy of every twig, spider web, leaf and blade of grass is only magnified by Jack Frost's cold touch. And while the sun shines brightly, it's not strong enough to thaw and we are, for a few hours, lucky enough to bask in nature's magical winter wonderland.

SWEEP UP LEAVES

Now that autumn foliage has fallen, sweep up the last leaves from paths and patios where they'll soon become slippery. Any that have fallen on borders can be left to break down in the soil.

SHOP FOR SEEDS

Spend a rainy afternoon shopping for easy-grow seeds to sow outside in spring. In March, sprinkle them onto trays of moist Westland Seed Trays Compost (£3.95/10- litres, diy. com), and cover with a thin layer of compost. Place on your windowsill, then when the seedlings have at least three leaves, plant into bigger pots and move outside in late spring.

Simple steps to keep your plot looking good this season

WARM UP YOUR SUMMER HOUSE

A cheap and easy way to insulate it is to use bubblewrap (£10.23/750mm x 25m, kitepackaging.co.uk). Just cut to fit, overlap the edges and tack MDF boards over the top. If your summerhouse has electric wiring, go for a foil-based compressed insulation instead such as Thermawall (£17/1200 x 450 x 100mm, wickes.co.uk), fixed on top of a breathable membrane with plywood board on top.

SHAPE UP TREES

If your trees and shrubs are taking over, now's the time to tidy them up. Cutting them back too much can mean a loss of flowers and berries for a few years and can spoil their natural shape. Instead, raise the canopy by removing several lower branches back to the main trunk. This allows extra light to reach the soil below so you can add some low-growing plants underneath.

PLANT A HELLEBORE

A Christmas rose will bloom in winter amid frost, snow and rain, cheering your garden all the way into May. It'll shine in a pot or at the front of a border in sun or partial shade and can be planted now just as long as the soil isn't frozen.

AVOID SOGGY ROOTS

Remove any saucers in winter so pots can free-drain but don't put your watering can away as plants may still need water during rain-free spells if the compost starts to dry out.

BRIGHTEN UP GREY DAYS

For a festive-looking display, plant a winter-flowering cherry for a burst of blossom from December to March. 'Autumnalis' (£83.99, ornamental-trees.co.uk) is perfect for a small space as it only grows to a height of 4m in 20 years.

CLEAN GUTTERS

Leaves in gutters will block the flow of water and, if they're washed into your waterbutt, will sink and eventually make it smelly. Disconnect the downpipe from your waterbutt, then use a hose to wash them through.

FRESHEN UP BIRCH TREES

To make the white stems and trunk really stand out, peel off any loose, flaky bark. In damp weather green algae can grow on the white bark, which spoils the effect. To brighten it up, head out with a bucket of water and a scrubbing brush and give the trunk a good wash down to make it shine.

Breezy walks and cosy pubs

Work up an appetite for hearty pub grub, on a crisp winter's walk

There's nothing nicer on a frosty morning than heading out into the British countryside for a ramble... that is, unless it's followed by a delicious meal or a tipple in a cosy pub! Wrap up warm and don't let the weather get in the way of your daily constitutional.

SEA BREEZE

For a blustery walk with a warm ending, head out from the National Trust car park in Rhossili Bay, in Swansea, and follow the trail parallel to the beach.

There's a pleasant five-mile route that's dog-friendly and takes in the 12th Century St Mary's Church, stunning views from Rhossili Down, a Second World War radar station, and even the site of a Bronze-Age cairn that was built four thousand years ago!

There's a café at the half-way point (Eddie's Café) and you can rest your feet (or your head!) at the end with a visit to The Worm's Head Hotel, which has a comfortable lounge offering sea views and food from midday until 9pm.

■ For a full route description, visit nationaltrust.org.uk/trails/rhosili-down-hillend-and-beach-walk

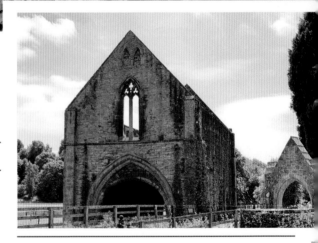

ABBEY DAYS

The George and Dragon, in Hudswell, North Yorkshire, is a multi-award-winning establishment that brews its own beer in the barn next door, and offers a range of popular pies. Burn off that pastry with an ambitious seven-mile loop out to Easby Abbey, an English Heritage-protected ruin with free entry, that was a favourite subject for the painter JMW Turner. Shorter routes are also a great option, including along the banks of the rushing River Swale.

■ Contact the George and Dragon on 01748 518373 or visit georgeanddragonhudswell.co.uk
■ For information on Easby Abbey, visit english-heritage.org.uk

A PINT OF HISTORY

The Fleece Inn, Bretforton, Worcestershire, has been serving drinks since 1848, so it would be rude not to indulge in a tipple and some locally sourced delights by the fireplace.

You can even stay the night in the National Trust-owned pub too. There are lots of walks nearby, including the Cotswold Way National Trail, which can be joined at Chipping Camden, Broadway Tower, which is an incredible viewpoint, or the National Trust's Hidcote, an Arts and Crafts-inspired garden that's sure to delight anyone with green fingers.

■ For more information about the Fleece Inn, visit thefleeceinn.co.uk or call 01386 831173.
■ For information on Hidcote, call 01386 438333

A SMUGGLER'S DREAM

Indulge your childhood fantasies of smugglers and pirates with a trip to the Tiger Inn, East Dean, East Sussex. Not only is it the snuggest of winter spots (think oak beams and open fire), but it has a history of serving ales and food to smugglers (and everyone else) since the 16th Century.

There's an easy loop to and from the pub, including sea views with a glimpse of Belle Tout lighthouse, and the South Downs Way, perfect for working up an appetite for sausage and mash or a warming casserole.

■ For a full route, visit nationaltrust.org.uk/birling-gap-and-the-seven-sisters

CITY SIGHTS

When you think of pub walks, it's likely you imagine the countryside, but there are equally great combinations in cities if you know where to look. Edinburgh's highest point – Arthur's Seat – is an ancient volcano, which makes for a challenging yet satisfying climb. The best part is, it won't take very long – roughly two hours – yet provides incredible views over the city. You're spoilt for choice when it comes to post-walk pubs, but the award-winning Pickles, on Broughton Street, takes some beating. It's a wine bar, softly lit with candles and fairy lights, and filled with intimate nooks and crannies.

■ For Pickles call 07485 711023 or find out more at www.getpickled.co.uk

What a cracker!

These fun and bright table decorations can be personalised for each guest

1 Begin by sticking a piece of double-sided tape on to your ready-made cracker, then carefully roll the paper being sure not to cause any creases.

2 Cut off any excess paper so that it is flush to the cracker and carefully begin twisting and squeezing the paper in to the joining areas.

3 Use your chosen ribbon to pull the paper together, creating a cracker formation. Be careful not to pull too tight, too quickly as you don't want to make the paper tear.

4 Repeat this process on both ends of the cracker/cardboard tube.

5 Now you can create a fun, colourful and bold style using crêpe paper and stickers. Cut out lengths of the paper measured to the diameter of the end of your cracker tube. You'll need two pieces per cracker.

6 Attach double-sided tape around the top of the opening and peel off. Then, roll up your piece of crêpe paper, put it inside the end of the cracker then carefully unroll it whilst sticking it to the tape.

7 Cut off any excess paper to the length you wish to overlap.

8 Create as many crackers in as many colours as you wish.
  Once that's complete, it's time to have some fun with stickers! Use them to create festive slogans or words, or even use them to personalise your cracker for your guests by adding their name.

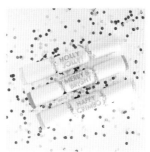

9 We used catchy phrases such as 'Holly Jolly' and 'Merry & Bright', but the decision is up to you!

You will need...
Double-sided sticky tape
Scissors
6 fillable crackers
White post display roll paper (76cm x 10m)
Silver ribbon
Assorted crêpe paper (100cm x 50cm)
Gold foil foam letter stickers
Rose gold foam alphabet stickers
ALL MATERIALS AVAILABLE FROM HOBBYCRAFT.CO.UK

Notable dates 2023

New Year's Day (Bank Holiday observed)	Monday January 2
Bank Holiday (Scotland)	Tuesday January 3
Epiphany	Friday January 6
Chinese New Year (Rabbit)	Sunday January 22
Burns' Night	Wednesday January 25
Valentine's Day	Tuesday February 14
Shrove Tuesday (Pancake Day)	Tuesday February 21
Ash Wednesday	Wednesday February 22
St David's Day	Wednesday March 1
St Patrick's Day (Bank Holiday N. Ireland/Eire)	Friday March 17
Mothering Sunday	Sunday March 19
First Day of Ramadan (Islam)	Wednesday March 22
British Summer Time begins (clocks go forward)	Sunday March 26
Palm Sunday	Sunday April 2
First Day of Passover (Jewish Holiday)	Wednsday April 5
Maundy Thursday	Thursday April 6
Good Friday (Bank Holiday)	Friday April 7
Easter Sunday	Sunday April 9
Easter Monday (Bank Holiday)	Monday April 10
St George's Day	Sunday April 23
May Day (Early May Bank Holiday)	Monday May 1
Ascension Day	Thursday May 18
Spring Bank Holiday	Monday May 29
Fathers' Day	Sunday June 18
Summer Solstice (Longest day)	Wednesday June 21
Armed Forces Day	Saturday June 24
American Independence Day	Tuesday July 4
Battle of the Boyne (Holiday N. Ireland)	Wednesday July 12
St Swithun's Day	Saturday July 15
Islamic New Year	Tuesday July 18
Summer Bank Holiday (Scotland / Eire)	Monday August 7
Summer Bank Holiday	Monday August 28
Jewish New Year (Rosh Hashanah)	Friday September 15
Trafalgar Day	Saturday October 21
British Summer Time ends (clocks go back)	Sunday October 29
Hallowe'en	Tuesday October 31
All Saints' Day	Wednesday November 1
Guy Fawkes' Night	Sunday November 5
Remembrance Sunday	Sunday November 12
Diwali (Hindu Festival)	Sunday November 12
First Sunday in Advent	Sunday December 3
Winter Solstice (Shortest day)	Friday December 22
St Andrew's Day	Thursday November 30
Christmas Day	Monday December 25
Boxing Day	Tuesday December 26
New Year's Eve/Hogmanay	Sunday December 31

THE YEAR AHEAD

1 SUNDAY

2 MONDAY

3 TUESDAY

4 WEDNESDAY

5 THURSDAY

6 FRIDAY

7 SATURDAY

Precious memories

SLIP SLIDING AWAY

As we remember the sixtieth anniversary of the big freeze of 1962-63, I thought you'd like to see how my sister and I became the envy of our friends that winter. We knew Dad had a secret project on the go when we were not allowed into the shed and could hear sawing and drilling going on behind the closed door.

Dad always had a stash of pieces of wood kept because one day he'd find a use for them. And when the big reveal came, he excelled himself. He stood back with pride to show us his late Christmas present to us – our very own sledge. It was dark green (left-over paint from our back gate) with Cresta Run in white emblazoned on the sides. It had stainless steel runners to glide through the snow more easily and plenty of room for two.

On with our gloves and wellies, we took turns to tow it to a hill nearby. I still remember the thrill as we gained speed, shrieking as we flew along. If only we'd learned how to stop!

Expensive presents aren't always the best. This one was made with love from odds and ends and it meant the world to us.

Claire Waite, Retford

Quick puzzle

Can you unscramble this 9-letter conundrum to form a word? You'll find the answer below.

TYRMANOME

A: MOMENTARY

Time for you

Start a happiness jar

Write down every time something good happens or you are grateful and pop it in a jar. This is your happiness jar. Continue this throughout 2023 and then you'll have wonderful memories to reflect on at the end of the year.

What a good idea!

If you plan to make a New Year's Resolution, make sure you choose something that's specific and measurable. So instead of saying, 'this year I'm going to get fit', try saying, 'this year I'm going to join a walking club to get fit'. Most importantly, make sure your goal is achievable!

Box office blockbusters!

Doris Day recorded Secret Love for Calamity Jane (1953) in just one take – it went on to top the charts and won an Oscar for Best Original Song. Her performance also went on to inspire the character of Jessie in the Toy Story films!

Recipe of the week

WALNUT ZA'ATAR FLATBREADS

Serves: 4
Prep: 2 hours
Cook: 12 mins

For the flatbread dough:
220g (8oz) white flour
½ tsp salt
½ tsp sugar
1 tsp fast action dried yeast
60ml (2½ fl oz) dairy-free milk
80ml (3 fl oz) water
1½ tbsp olive oil
For the topping:
50g (2oz) California Walnuts
5 tbsp olive oil
2 tbsp Za'atar mix
To serve:
4 tbsp lemon juice
Pomegranate seeds

1 In a large bowl, mix the flour, salt, sugar and yeast, then pour in the milk, water and olive oil. Knead for a few mins, then transfer to a bowl, cover with cling film and tea towels and leave in a warm place to rise. This should take 1-2 hours.
2 Punch the dough down and divide into 4 balls. Place onto a floured worktop and roll out with a rolling pin into a circle, then transfer the flatbreads onto a baking sheet lined with baking paper.
3 Mix the topping ingredients in a bowl (California Walnuts, olive oil and Za'atar mix) then spread over the flatbreads and bake in a preheated oven at 220°C/200°C Fan/Gas Mark 7 for 12 mins.
4 To serve, squeeze about 1 tbsp of fresh lemon juice on each and top with pomegranate seeds. Enjoy!
NADIA'S HEALTHY KITCHEN

8 SUNDAY

9 MONDAY

10 TUESDAY

11 WEDNESDAY

12 THURSDAY

13 FRIDAY

14 SATURDAY

Precious memories

GOODNIGHT, GIRLS!

Bedtimes in the Fifties were very cosy for us. After our cup of Horlicks or Ovaltine, up we trekked to our attic bedroom. I slept with my two little sisters in a double bed pushed up against the wall. We were like sardines packed tightly together. Our nighties were made from old sheets, Dad drew a design on each of them and Mum embroidered them. Mine had daffodils on it. Mum also made the dresses we are wearing in the photo.

While my sisters, Julie and Carole, teased each other or played with their dolls, I would read stories to them from a book or from the Beano, Dandy or Bunty comics. In wintertime it was so cold in the attic that our bedding was a heap of blankets, quilts and heavy coats piled on top of us.

It was too cold and too scary to walk to the outside toilet during the night so we used a large potty instead. In the morning Mum had to carry it down two flights of stairs to empty it in the creepy lavatory at the bottom of the garden. It was a dungeon-like room with whitewashed walls and a stone floor where spiders and woodlice abounded despite a daily brushdown.

Annie Rider, Cirencester

Time for you

Create an evening routine

An evening routine is great for winding down from the day and preparing your mind and body for sleep. This could include putting your phone away, having a night-time skincare routine, doing a late-night meditation or relaxing with a good book.

What a good idea!

Short of wardrobe space? Double up your hangers by placing a fizzy drink can ring pull over the neck of the hanger. Then simply thread another hanger through the other hole of the ring pull to create a double hanger that takes up less room.

Box office blockbusters!

On landing the title role in Cleopatra (1963), Elizabeth Taylor said: "If someone's dumb enough to offer me a million dollars to make a picture, I'm certainly not dumb enough to turn it down." Renegotiations meant she actually took home $7million (equivalent to £64.3m today!).

Recipe of the week

VEGAN CHOC BROWNIES

Serves: 16
Prep: 10 mins
Cook: 45 mins

250g (9oz) all-plain flour
1 tsp Bioglan Superfoods Cacao Boost
85g (3oz) unsweetened cocoa powder
200g (7oz) light brown sugar
200g (7oz) white granulated sugar
1 tsp baking powder
½ tsp salt
1 tbsp instant coffee
240ml (8 fl oz) vegan buttermilk (1 tbsp lemon juice + 240ml (8fl oz) soy milk)
240ml (8 fl oz) coconut oil, melted
1 tsp vanilla extract
115g (4oz) vegan chocolate, melted
175g (6oz) vegan chocolate chips and chunks (plus extra to place on top)

1 Preheat the oven to 180°C/160°C Fan/Gas Mark 4. Line a 9 x 9in square dish with baking parchment.
2 Sift the flour, Bioglan Superfood Cacao Boost and cocoa powder into a mixing bowl. Then add the brown and white sugar, baking powder, salt and instant coffee powder and mix.
3 Prepare your vegan buttermilk by adding 1 tbsp of lemon juice to a measuring jug and then adding the soy milk up to the 240ml (8 fl oz) line. Allow it to curdle and then add to the mixing bowl.
4 Add the melted coconut oil and vanilla extract and stir it into a thick batter. Pour in the melted vegan chocolate and stir. Fold in the melted chocolate chips and chunks. Spoon the batter out into the prepared baking dish and smooth down with the back of a spoon. Place the extra chocolate chunks and chocolate chips on top.
5 Bake for 30 mins. Cool on a wire rack.
BIOGLAN SUPERFOODS

15 SUNDAY

16 MONDAY

17 TUESDAY

18 WEDNESDAY

19 THURSDAY

20 FRIDAY

21 SATURDAY

Precious memories

MY HARD-WORKING DAD

This is a photo of me with my dear father, William, known as Billy. He was very hard working, sometimes doing other work as well as a full-time job to provide for me and my mother. He saved up to buy a house when most people in the area were renting. Growing up, I lived in several houses as my parents moved up the property ladder thanks to my dad's renovations.

Although he had a clever mind, he didn't have the benefit of a good education, but he would try his hand at anything. For a time he worked as a coalman and sometimes he would do 'flittings' (house removals). He was the one who taught me to read and to swim. He even made many of my dresses on a sewing machine. He loved animals and kept hens and pigs – even a donkey.

As an only child, my parents always wanted the best for me, but they were also generous to those who were less well off than they were. My father passed on to me the belief that most problems are solvable if you are determined enough, so if I struggle with something I still ask for his help and usually find the answer.
Janet Dandy, Burnley

Quick puzzle

Can you unscramble this 9-letter conundrum to form a word? You'll find the answer below.

SLRMKHAAL

A: HALLMARKS

Time for you

Try birdwatching

Looking at the feathery friends fluttering around your garden has been shown to lower the risk of anxiety, stress and depression, so take time in your day to factor in some birdwatching. You can even get involved in the RSPB Big Garden Birdwatch at the end of the month.

What a good idea!

Staying motivated and sticking to your January keep fit goals can be tough. Why not try downloading a gripping audio book and only allowing yourself to listen to it while exercising? The prospect of a good cliff hanger should be enough motivation to get you moving.

Box office blockbusters!

Yul Brynner starred in the long-running smash hit Broadway play The King and I, playing the King a staggering 4,633 times before taking on the role in the 1956 film version. No wonder he went on to win an Oscar for the part!

Recipe of the week

NO BAKE CHOCOLATE & CHERRY GRANOLA BARS

Serves: 12
Prep: 15 mins
Cook: None

80ml (3oz) maple syrup
100g (4oz) almond butter
130g (5oz) Flahavan's Organic Jumbo Oats
190g (7oz) dates, stoned
200g (7oz) toasted blanched hazelnuts
100g (4oz) dried sour cherries
60g (2oz) dark chocolate buttons, roughly chopped
30g (10z) ground flaxseed

1 Line a 20cm square loose bottom brownie tin with baking parchment.
2 In a small saucepan, gently warm the maple syrup and almond butter until smooth and combined.
3 Meanwhile, tip half the hazelnuts into a food processor and process until finely ground. Add to a large mixing bowl with the oats. Then, roughly chop the remaining hazelnuts and add these into the mixing bowl.
4 Add the dates to the food processor and process until finely chopped and they come together into one ball. Then, add these, the maple syrup and peanut butter to the mixing bowl, along with the remaining ingredients. Stir and, once combined, use your hands to bring the mixture together.
5 Tip the mixture into your prepared tin and press into an even layer using the back of a spoon. Chill in the fridge for 20-30 mins, before slicing into bars.

22 SUNDAY

23 MONDAY

24 TUESDAY

25 WEDNESDAY

26 THURSDAY

27 FRIDAY

28 SATURDAY

Precious memories

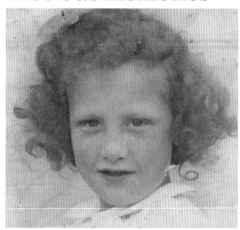

SONGS OF PRAISE

As a little girl I attended the Primitive Methodist Church at Ladmanlow, a small village by a limestone quarry. I loved going to Sunday School and remember all the teachers with gratitude.

We started every week with our preacher, Mr Plant, giving us a little sermon followed by lots of hymn-singing which I loved and still know all the words off by heart. Among my favourite hymns were Jesus Bids Us Shine and New Every Morning Is The Love. Then we went into a smaller room where there was a large tray of sand with some cardboard figures of characters from the Bible. Miss Bentley used to tell us a story and we created the scene using the figures. If the weather was fine we went for a walk in the afternoon after we had been home for dinner.

We had an annual Sunday School trip as well as a Christmas party which our parents helped to organise. The Chapel Anniversary was also a very special day for us children when we stood on a small stage and sang, accompanied by the organ.

After my marriage I was baptised into the Anglican church and for many years was a member of the choir at St Peter's church in Fairfield.

Margery Sherwood, Buxton

Quick puzzle

Can you unscramble this 9-letter conundrum to form a word? You'll find the answer below.

RAIWDHOKN

A: HANDIWORK

Time for you

Give alphabet dating a go

Get creative and take turns with your partner to plan regular date nights where you work through the alphabet in order to plan your activity. For example, A might be Afternoon tea or Aquarium while B could be Bingo or Breakfast.

What a good idea!

Having a bit of a move around, or a furniture upgrade? Get rid of furniture dents in your carpet with this simple ice-cube trick. Place the cube over the dent and leave it to melt. Once dry, vacuum the area for a carpet that looks good as new.

Box office blockbusters!

We have The Bee Gees to thank not just for their disco soundtrack to Saturday Night Fever (1977) but for the name of the film. Originally known as Tribal Rites of the New Saturday Night, it was changed when The Bee Gees submitted the song Night Fever.

Recipe of the week

SPICY COCONUT NOODLES

Serves: 2
Prep: 5 mins
Cook: 25 mins

200g (7oz) noodles
Spice paste:
25g (1oz) ginger, peeled
3 cloves garlic
2 red chillies
2 stalks lemongrass
1 tsp coriander seeds
1 tsp ground turmeric
Splash of vegetable oil
For the noodle sauce:
1-2 diced onions
130g-150g (5oz) mushrooms
500ml (17 fl oz) vegetable stock
400ml (14 fl oz) coconut milk
200g (7oz) spinach
100g (3oz) deep fried tofu puffs
Fresh coriander
Fresh lime juice

1 Cook the noodles according to the instructions on the packet, drain and set aside.
2 Blend the spice paste in a high-speed blender or food processor.
3 In a large saucepan or wok, fry the spice blend for a few mins. Add the onion and mushrooms.
4 Stir through and heat for a further few mins.
5 Add the stock and coconut milk, bring to the boil and then simmer for 10-15 mins.
6 Add the spinach, tofu and the noodles and simmer for a further minute.
7 Remove from the heat (do not drain) and serve with fresh coriander and a squeeze of lime juice.
VEGAN RECIPE CLUB

29 SUNDAY

30 MONDAY

31 TUESDAY

1 WEDNESDAY

2 THURSDAY

3 FRIDAY

4 SATURDAY

Precious memories

A JANUARY WEDDING

When the vicar asked me the date I wished to get married, I knew immediately – Saturday, January 29. The reason for choosing this day was that it was the date Charles Darwin married Emma Wedgwood at the parish church of St Peter at Maer in Staffordshire and, 183 years later, James and I wanted to do the same.

We both had sentimental connections with the area. James was born in nearby Market Drayton. My grandmother, Hannah Foxley, worked in service at Maer Hall and my father is buried in the churchyard. More recently, during the Covid lockdown, I joined in with church services by Zoom from my home in Fife.

We chose to wear Regency wedding outfits. I wore an ivory silk Empire line dress with a pale green jacket, a rose-pink velvet cloak and lace-up boots. James complemented me with his black frock coat and damask red-and-black waistcoat. His winged-collar shirt and cravat were specially made for him by a friend.

In January 2022 we were lucky enough to enjoy perfect weather for the happiest day of our lives. Friends and family joined our celebrations. There is always hope of finding true love, as we did at the ages of sixty-seven and seventy-two.
Carol Ann Massey, Ceres, Cupar

Quick puzzle
Can you unscramble this 9-letter conundrum to form a word? You'll find the answer below.

VEEEGERRN

A: EVERGREEN

Time for you

Up your Vitamin D

It may be vital for your bones, muscles and immune system, but as a UK resident you're unlikely to get enough Vitamin D from sunshine. Add sources of Vitamin D to your diet such as oily fish, liver, eggs and fortified foods including breakfast cereals or supplements.

What a good idea!

Pick up a pen every time you eat and note down the time and what you're eating. Keeping a record of everything you eat is useful for spotting bad habits. It's also handy for helping to highlight any foods that trigger unpleasant side-effects.

Box office blockbusters!

The sound of snakes slithering in Indiana Jones and the Raiders of the Lost Ark (1981) was created by sound designer Ben Burtt running his fingers through a cheese casserole. "It gives a real oily, mushy sound. If you can record that and build it up in several layers, you can give a nice sense of slimy snakes."

Recipe of the week

ROAST CAULIFLOWER SALAD WITH HONEY & MUSTARD DRESSING

Serves: 4
Prep: 10 mins
Cook: 40-45 mins

For the salad:
1 head of cauliflower
1 can chickpeas, drained and rinsed
Extra-virgin olive oil
1 tsp cumin
2 tsp paprika
Pinch of salt
3 cloves garlic, minced
Handful mixed lettuce leaves
½ cucumber, sliced
3 tbsp fresh dill, roughly chopped
3 tbsp fresh parsley, roughly chopped
2 tbsp fresh chives, finely chopped
150g (5oz) feta cheese
For the dressing:
3 tbsp extra-virgin olive oil
3 tbsp Comvita UMF 5+ Mānuka Honey
2 tbsp Dijon mustard
½ tbsp white wine vinegar
Juice of half a lemon
Pinch of salt

1 Preheat the oven to 180°C/160°C Fan/Gas Mark 4 and line a tray with baking paper.
2 Cut the cauliflower into small florets and place on the tray. Add the chickpeas to the tray and drizzle with a generous amount of oil.
3 Sprinkle the cumin, paprika, salt and garlic over the cauliflowers and chickpeas and toss to coat. Cook for 40-45 mins.
4 Assemble the salad by placing the lettuce leaves, cucumber, and herbs in a bowl.
5 Prepare the dressing by placing all dressing ingredients into a jar and shaking to combine.
6 Once cooked, add the cauliflower and chickpeas to the bowl. Crumble the feta on top of the salad and gently toss through the dressing.

COMVITA MANUKA HONEY AND NUTRITIONIST RACHEL HAWKINS

5 SUNDAY

6 MONDAY

7 TUESDAY

8 WEDNESDAY

9 THURSDAY

10 FRIDAY

11 SATURDAY

Precious memories

BRRR..!

Who could forget the very cold winter of 1962-63? It started to snow on Boxing Day; the temperature dropped and stayed below freezing for three months. Our son was only six months old and it was not possible to take him out in his pushchair for all that time as the pavements were solid ice. The River Medway froze and I recall holding him up and saying: "Look, the river is frozen" (although how much a small baby was able to take in I don't know!).

Without the luxury of double glazing and central heating that we enjoy today, it was cold indoors as well. 'Jack Frost' made pretty patterns on the window panes. I used drawing pins to attach the sides of the curtains to the window frames to stop the draught blowing in. It was so cold that milk froze in the bottle, pushing up the lid. Even the water in the toilet froze.

Hot water bottles were definitely needed and underclothes were put under the pillow at night so they would be warm enough to put on in the morning. I remember, too, how painful chilblains were. It was such a relief when the temperature began to rise in March and it was possible to walk outside again.

Annette Morgan, Gillingham

Quick puzzle
Can you unscramble this 9-letter conundrum to form a word? You'll find the answer below.

IENIDISTG

A: DIGNITIES

Time for you

Try journaling

This is a valuable tool that can help you focus your thoughts and feelings, and notice habits and problems that you can solve. By putting pen to paper and spilling your mind onto the page, you can use your journal to set goals, reflect on your day or just let out any pent up angst.

What a good idea!

In need of a wardrobe detox? Why not organise a clothes swap get-together with friends. Take along any clothes from your wardrobe that don't fit or flatter. Have fun trying on your friend's fashion cast offs and take home some fresh new pieces for your own wardrobe – for free!

Box office blockbusters!

When To Sir, With Love (1967) did so unexpectedly well in the US, Columbia Pictures completed market research to discover why. The answer was simple: it was thanks to Sidney Poitier. Luckily, he'd secured 10 per cent of the box office, and made the equivalent of $45m!

Recipe of the week

LAMB MEATBALLS WITH GRANA PADANO & YOGURT

Serves: 6
Prep: 15 mins
Cook: 45 mins

Tomato sauce:
1 tbsp olive oil
1 large onion, finely chopped
½ garlic clove, finely chopped
400g (14oz) fresh or tinned plum tomatoes, chopped
2 tbsp tomato purée
For the meatballs:
700g (1 ½lb) lamb mince
200g (7oz) bread
500ml (17fl oz) milk
Salt, to taste
Pepper, to taste
100g (3oz) Grana Padano Riserva, grated

10g (½oz) parsley, chopped
10g (½oz) basil, chopped
½ clove garlic, chopped

Chardonnay (or white wine) vinegar
15g (½oz) N`duja (spicy sausage from Calabria)
For the garnish:
1 tbsp capers
12 anchovies
25g (1oz) Grana Padano Riserva, grated
300ml (10 fl oz) natural yogurt
500g (17oz) Swiss chard leaves

1 Start by making the tomato sauce. Heat the oil in a large pan over a gentle heat. Add the onion and garlic and cook very gently for about 10 mins until soft. Then add the tomatoes and tomato purée and season. Stir, then leave to simmer for a further 20 mins.

2 To make the meatballs, combine all the meatball ingredients together in a mixing bowl. Then make the individual balls which should be around 30-40g (1-1½oz) each and, once all ready, place them in the simmering tomato sauce to cook. Add the vinegar and n`duja and and cook for 15 mins. While this is happening blanch the swiss chard leaves in boiling salted water for 30 secs.

3 Plate up and add anchovies and the swiss chard leaves on the top, then sprinkle with grated Grana Padano Riserva and serve with yogurt and capers on the side, adding to taste.

GRANA PADANO

12 SUNDAY

13 MONDAY

14 TUESDAY

15 WEDNESDAY

16 THURSDAY

17 FRIDAY

18 SATURDAY

Precious memories

MY FIRST VALENTINE

Mick and I met when the Ranger Guides were invited to Moreton-in-Marsh Youth Club disco and Mum let me go! I was fifteen years old and felt very smart in my Op Art black shift dress with a broad orange stripe at the hem. I had sneaked out a pair of my sister's shoes with small heels (Mum's idea of shoes was black lace-ups for winter and T-bar sandals for summer).

Mick was with a group of friends who were egging him on to ask me to dance. Eventually he did. Outside, we shared a kiss to The Searchers singing Needles and Pins. It was magical.

Soon after this it was Valentine's Day. I put my phone number in a card which bore the words 'I'll know you love me true if I receive a ring from you'. Mick did ring and we took our romance from there. We went for walks down Cotswold lanes and if the weather was inclement we went to a pub where I broke the law by having half a pint of cider.

When I started training to be a nurse, I felt it wasn't fair to keep him dangling so, sadly, I said farewell. I later heard he was married with a family. C'est la vie.

Diana Mansell, Grantham

Quick puzzle

Can you unscramble this 9-letter conundrum to form a word? You'll find the answer below.

ESSEOTMCY

A: ECOSYSTEM

Time for you

Manage your stress

Stress can be overwhelming and hard to come down from. To help you feel calmer, create a to-do list with small achievable goals to break down what seems like the insurmountable.

What a good idea!

Use the TV advert breaks to get things done! Whether it's seizing the opportunity to get some steps in and exercise, or do some jobs. Try washing up, folding and putting away some laundry, or organising a cupboard in super-quick time.

Box office blockbusters!

Shirley MacLaine and Debra Winger fell out on the set of Terms of Endearment (1983), but when they were both nominated for the Best Actress Oscar and MacLaine won, she whispered to Winger "Half of this belongs to you." Winger agreed and replied "I'll take half!"

Recipe of the week

DARK CHOCOLATE & CHERRY COOKIES

Serves: 6-8
Prep: 15 mins
Cook: 10 mins

115g (4oz) Plain flour
30g (1oz) best quality cocoa powder
½ tsp salt
¼ tsp baking powder
225g (8oz) best quality dark chocolate, roughly chopped
130g (5oz) unsalted butter
2 eggs
130g (5oz) caster sugar
1 tsp vanilla extract
1 jar Opies cocktail cherries, drained and cherries halved

1 Preheat the oven to 200°C/180° Fan/Gas Mark 4. Line a large baking tray and set aside.
2 Sift the flour, cocoa powder, salt and baking powder into a bowl.
3 Place a pan of water on the hob and boil. Place 175g (6oz) of the chocolate and butter in a heatproof bowl then place on top of the saucepan, don't let it touch the water. Stir through until the chocolate and butter is melted then remove and leave to cool.
4 Using a bowl or stand mixer, beat the eggs and sugar together until pale and light. Add the vanilla and melted chocolate mixture and gently mix again until just combined.
5 Next add the flour mixture and stir through until the mixture is even and chocolatey in colour.
6 Add golf-ball sized spoonfuls of cake batter onto the lined baking tray, spaced about 3cm (1in) apart, and shape the mounds into hearts using moistened fingertips. Press cherry halves cut-side down into the mixture then bake in the pre-heated oven for 10 mins.
7 Remove and leave to rest for 5 mins until cool enough to handle. Transfer to a wire rack to cool completely then melt the remaining 50g (2oz) of chocolate in a saucepan and drizzle over the biscuits before leaving to set. Enjoy!
WWW.OPIESFOODS.COM

19 SUNDAY

20 MONDAY

21 TUESDAY

SHROVE TUESDAY (PANCAKE DAY)

22 WEDNESDAY

ASH WEDNESDAY (LENT)
(FAST?)

23 THURSDAY

24 FRIDAY

25 SATURDAY

Precious memories

RACING FOR CHARITY

This photo of our pancake race in Wrexham was taken on Shrove Tuesday, 1980 – I am on the right, wearing a chef's hat. The runners were from the town's shops and had been invited to take part in support of their own chosen charities.

I was the manager of a busy bookmaker's shop at the time, but on this day I was just a bookie's runner! The event attracted a good-sized crowd to cheer their favourite competitors. The route was a straight up and down race, taking us back to the starting line.

Despite it being a fun event there were race stewards to watch out for any skulduggery such as keeping thumbs on pancakes or insufficient pancake tossing. First to finish was the young man in a shower cap (fourth from left) who, judging by his T-shirt, was representing Boots the chemist. He certainly showed the rest of us a clean pair of heels.

Since then I have taken part in many events to raise funds for charity from nineteen Great North Runs, four London Marathons and one parachute jump.
John Nicholls, Sedgefield

Quick puzzle
Can you unscramble this 9-letter conundrum to form a word? You'll find the answer below.

NTIIBDHIE

A: INHIBITED

Time for you

Do a good turn
Not only does volunteering help bring people closer together, but by dedicating time to others, you can boost your self-esteem and life satisfaction. Work on something that's meaningful to you or help a neighbour with their shopping – a helping hand goes a long way.

What a good idea!

It's a favourite pancake topping, but the humble lemon is also a superstar when it comes to cleaning your home. Great at getting rid of limescale, rub a halved lemon over your tap and areas of limescale build up. Leave for ten minutes, before scrubbing gently with a toothbrush and rinsing.

Box office blockbusters!

From Here to Eternity (1953) won a staggering eight Oscars but the passionate beach scene with Burt Lancaster and Deborah Kerr, which helped to make it a classic, wasn't originally planned. The waves hitting them was a last-minute call from the director.

Recipe of the week

NUTTY BANANA CHOCOLATE CHIP PANCAKES

Serves: 10
Prep: 20 mins
Cook: 3 mins

120g (4oz) packet pancake mix
240ml (8 fl oz) milk
85g (30z) SKIPPY® Smooth Peanut Butter
½ large banana, chopped
55g (2oz) plain chocolate chips
30g (1oz) chopped walnuts
2 tsp ground cinnamon
1 large egg
Syrup, if desired

1 In a medium bowl, combine all the ingredients except the syrup; mix until blended.
2 Coat a 30cm non-stick frying pan with oil spray. Heat over a medium-low heat. Scoop 30ml of batter into the pan; cook, turning once, until the pancakes are golden brown. Repeat with the remaining batter. Serve with favourite syrup, if desired.
SKIPPY®

26 SUNDAY

27 MONDAY

28 TUESDAY

1 WEDNESDAY

2 THURSDAY

3 FRIDAY

4 SATURDAY

Precious memories

WATERCRESS AND WINKLES

My biological father, who was in the fire service, left my mother four weeks before I was born. Some months later she met the man that I call my dad. He was a hardworking labourer who would come home on a Friday night, take a few shillings from his pay packet for a couple of beers, and give the rest to my mother.

From when I was about ten years old on Saturday afternoons in the winter (when there was an R in the month) I would go with him to collect two buckets of winkles which we took home to wash and cook. The next day we would take them round the houses to sell at sixpence a pint.

Come spring we would collect watercress from the drainage ditch at Shoreham airport. We washed and bunched it and on Sunday mornings we'd sell it for sixpence a bunch. In autumn we used to walk for miles on the South Downs collecting mushrooms to hawk around the houses.

This Sunday morning ritual was for Dad's lunchtime beer with his mates at the pub. He always brought a bottle of stout back for Mum. For some reason (I never knew why) his mates called him Basil although his name was Arthur.

Robert Hunt, Brighton

Quick puzzle

Can you unscramble this 9-letter conundrum to form a word? You'll find the answer below.

DEIUSDNSM

A: MUDDINESS

Time for you

Try rose essential oil

Studies have shown that the use of rose oil can help to decrease blood pressure, heart rates and cortisol levels. Put a couple of drops of rose essential oil on your hands and inhale, or even wear a couple of drops as a fragrance.

What a good idea!

Make pots for seedlings out of eggshells. Crack your eggs so you have a good portion of the shell intact. Wash and make a hole with a pin in the bottom then place the shell inside the egg carton and plant your seed. When ready, plant straight into the ground.

Box office blockbusters!

West Side Story (1961) won ten of the 11 Oscars it was nominated for, including Best Picture, which made it the highest Oscar-winning musical of all time. Rita Morena won Best Supporting Actress for her role as Anita and appears in the 2021 version.

Recipe of the week

CHICKEN TAGINE

Serves: 6
Prep: 10 mins
Cook: 55 mins

12 chicken thighs, with the skin and bone intact
3 tsp harissa spice
3 tbsp olive oil
2 onions, thinly sliced
4 garlic cloves, thinly sliced
1tsp turmeric
½ tsp chilli flakes
1 tsp cumin
2 Opies Stem Ginger balls, finely chopped
1 cinnamon stick
400g (14oz) chickpeas, drained
500ml (17 fl oz) chicken stock
400g (14oz) chopped tomatoes
10 Opies lemon slices
10 apricots, halved

1 Marinate the chicken thighs in the harissa with 1 tbsp of the olive oil, making sure that all the chicken is coated.
2 Meanwhile in a casserole pot add the remaining olive oil, onions and garlic and cook over a medium heat until soft and the onions are just starting to brown. Sprinkle in the turmeric, cumin and chilli flakes and continue to fry for 1 min. Next add the ginger, cinnamon, chickpeas and keep for another minute.
3 Add the tinned tomatoes, chicken stock and lemon, then turn the heat down and gently simmer.
4 Turn the oven on to 200°C/180°C Fan/Gas Mark 6.
5 Place the chicken onto a roasting tray and cook for 10 mins just to seal the chicken.
6 Carefully place the chicken into the tagine, along with any juices from the tray. Place the lid on the casserole pot and return the pot to the oven.
7 After 30 mins add the apricots and return to the oven for a further 15 mins. Serve with couscous, fresh chopped parsley and a little mint.
WWW.OPIESFOODS.COM

5 SUNDAY

6 MONDAY

7 TUESDAY

8 WEDNESDAY

9 THURSDAY

10 FRIDAY

11 SATURDAY

Precious memories

A FLY BY NIGHT

Having a sort out recently, I came across the key I'm holding in this picture and it took me right back to my twenty-first birthday. I was in pantomime with the John Tiller Girls at the New Theatre in Cardiff. I took part in the flying ballet that flew over the audience from the stage to the balcony. I loved doing this until one night one of the wires got caught in my costume and snapped, leaving me dangling like a trussed chicken on a single wire.

A first aid man at the back of the stalls dashed backstage to help me. I calmed down after the fright wore off and was told that I must go up again at the evening show or I would lose my confidence (rather like getting back on your bike after falling off). I plucked up my courage and flew again.

The 'key of the door' was made for me by the stage hands and was presented to me at the end of the show with a large bouquet of flowers. Happy Birthday was sung to me by everyone, including the audience. It was a twenty-first birthday I'll never forget.
Barbie Carson, Warminster

Quick puzzle

Can you unscramble this 9-letter conundrum to form a word? You'll find the answer below.

TNHGLSISO

A: SLINGSHOT

Time for you

Pick up a colouring book

Colouring has been prescribed to help people since the 1900s. Famous psychologist Carl Jung is thought to have been the first to suggest it, as he believed colouring would help people express deeper parts of their psyche and calm their minds.

What a good idea!

Tea bags soak up moisture, so popping them in your shoes overnight will help keep them fresh smelling. However, if your shoes are already pongy, try sprinkling bicarbonate of soda (baking soda) into them and leaving overnight. In the morning empty them out and any unpleasant odours will have vanished!

Box office blockbusters!

Back to the Future (1985) was the highest grossing film that year, earning $381.1m, even though Michael J Fox wasn't allowed to go on promotional tours. He was working on Family Ties and had to stick to the TV show's strict schedule (and film most of his movie scenes at night).

Recipe of the week

CARROT CAKE BLISS BALLS

Serves: 25
Prep: 10 mins
Cook: None

200g (7oz) California Walnuts toasted
80g (3oz) oats
50g (2oz) sunflower seeds
2 heaped tsp ground ginger
1 heaped tsp ground turmeric
Zest and juice of half an orange
130g (5oz) grated carrot
200g (7oz) medjool dates
60g (2oz) desiccated coconut

1 Place the California Walnuts, oats, sunflower seeds, ginger, turmeric and orange zest into a food processor and pulse until you have fine breadcrumbs. Add the carrot and dates and whizz again. Add in a little of the orange juice and blitz again, adding a little more orange juice if needed, until the mixture just comes together.
2 Roll the mixture into 25 balls. Place the coconut onto a plate or tray, and roll the balls to coat. Chill in the fridge or keep in your freezer until needed.

CALIFORNIA WALNUTS

12 SUNDAY

13 MONDAY

14 TUESDAY

15 WEDNESDAY

16 THURSDAY

17 FRIDAY

18 SATURDAY

Precious memories

HI-DE-HI, CAMPERS!

On a dark, dank day in March 1966, I set off on my first adventure. A gangly teenager, full of nervous anticipation, I became a cashier at the self-service till of Pontins in Blackpool. The work was hard but there was also a lot of laughter.

As in Hi-de-Hi, the tannoy would wake the campers every day with a tune and a rundown of events. There was a lot of excitement when England took on Germany in the World Cup. Everything came to a standstill as campers gathered round the televisions to watch with bated breath until the final whistle went and England had won. Everyone was buoyed up for the rest of the day.

Every weekend the Blue Coats put on a show in the theatre. Frank Carson was the compère and had the audience in stitches with his bawdy jokes and The Bachelors sang their well-known hits. Pontins had its own line dance which was taught to the new campers who were soon showing off their talents every evening.

We were all swept along by the holiday atmosphere. Six months flew by in the blink of an eye and I would not have missed it for the world. (I am the middle girl in the photo.)
Carol Ellis, via email

Quick puzzle

Can you unscramble this 9-letter conundrum to form a word? You'll find the answer below.

CDTNOUSIS

A: DISCOUNTS

Time for you

Adjust your room temperature

Sleep scientists believe that a slightly cool room contributes to good sleep, meaning your body temperature has the environment it needs for rest and regeneration. A colder room is thought to help you fall asleep in less time and sleep deeper so keep the thermostat somewhere between 16°C to 18°C.

What a good idea!

Old screws can be difficult to remove, particularly if the screw head is worn. Try placing a wide elastic band over the top of the screw head. Hold it in place and use your screwdriver as normal – the rubber will fill the damaged grooves as well as giving extra grip.

Box office blockbusters!

The chocolate river in Willy Wonka & the Chocolate Factory (1971) was made from 150,000 gallons of water, chocolate and cream – the latter of which "turned" by the end of filming, so it stank. Poor Michael Bollner, who played Augustus Gloop, had to repeatedly fall into it.

Recipe of the week

CARAMELISED ONION & GORGONZOLA TART

Serves: 10
Prep: 30 mins
Cook: 50 mins

1 sheet ready-rolled puff pastry
100g (4oz) unsalted butter
1 tbsp brown sugar
600g (1¼lb) white onions, thinly sliced
100g (4oz) gorgonzola, crumbled
4 thyme sprigs

1 Preheat your oven to 200°C/180°C Fan/Gas Mark 6. Roll out the pastry to the size of your lined baking tray and prick with a fork. Chill for 30 mins.
2 Meanwhile, melt your butter in a saucepan at a medium heat. Add in your onions and cook for 10 mins until they start to caramelise. Add in the sugar and cook for a further 20 mins, stirring frequently.
3 Spread the onions over the pastry and sprinkle with gorgonzola. Season with salt, pepper, and thyme.
4 Bake in the oven for 20-22 mins or until the crust is golden and the cheese is melted.
5 Allow to cool for 5 mins, serve and enjoy.
WREN KITCHENS

19 SUNDAY

MOTHERING SUNDAY

20 MONDAY

21 TUESDAY

22 WEDNESDAY

23 THURSDAY

24 FRIDAY

25 SATURDAY

Precious memories

MY BEST PAL

Being an only child until the age of seven, my playmate was my cat, Chinky, from the day he arrived as a kitten. I was so excited on that first morning, I was up at six and ran downstairs to tap on the door of the porch where he was sleeping. My dad appeared and told me to go back to bed!

Chinky was a very lovable cat, but he really did seem to have nine lives. He was knocked over by a car and sustained a broken leg. After that he was in plaster for several weeks. My mum helped him to walk by supporting him with a headscarf under his tummy.

On another occasion he got into a fight with a neighbouring cat and his tail was so badly bitten that most of it had to be amputated. However, he continued to be a very active cat – a bit too active for my grandparents when they came to babysit. Chinky decided to run up and down the dining room curtains, much to the frustration of my normally placid gran. He ended up falling down behind the bookcase from where he had to be rescued.

Looking at this photo reminds me of the happy times Chinky and I had together.
Sonia French, via email

Quick puzzle

Can you unscramble this 9-letter conundrum to form a word? You'll find the answer below.

AECLESCPT

A: SPECTACLE

Time for you

Declutter
You may not realise it but decluttering your home can give you more headspace, helping you to feel lighter and more focused. Pick three items from a space you want to clear such as your wardrobe, bookshelf or kitchen cabinet and give them away.

What a good idea!
Clean a grimy, narrow-necked vase with this tip. Add three tablespoons of uncooked rice and half fill with water. Add two tablespoons of white vinegar and a few drops of washing-up liquid. Mix, then leave to soak for a few hours. Give it a good swirl around, then rinse.

Box office blockbusters!

Phileas Fogg might have done it in less than three months, but the making of 1956 epic Around the World in 80 Days actually involved cast and crew flying enough to circumnavigate the globe roughly 160 times (more than four million miles)!

Recipe of the week

CORNISH CLOTTED CREAM & LEMON DRIZZLE BUNDT CAKE

Serves: 10
Prep: 10 mins
Cook: 1 hour

450g (1lb) caster sugar
4 medium free range eggs
Finely grated zest and juice of 4 lemons
500g (1lb) Rodda's Cornish clotted cream
30ml (1fl oz) Rodda's Cornish milk
400g (14oz) self raising flour
Lemon drizzle:
4 tbsp granulated sugar
Zest and juice of 4 lemons

1 Preheat the oven to 180°C/160°C Fan/Gas Mark 4. Beat the caster sugar and eggs in a large bowl until light and fluffy and doubled in size.
2 In a separate bowl grate the lemon zest and squeeze in the juice, add the Rodda's clotted cream and stir together.
3 Gently beat in the clotted cream and lemon mix into the sugar and eggs, then add the milk. Sift the flour and gently fold into the mixture until well combined.
4 Spoon the mixture into a lightly oiled bundt tin (25x25x9cm) and level off the top. Bake the bundt cake for 45 mins to 1 hour or until a skewer inserted into the centre of the cake comes out clean.
5 Remove from the oven and leave the cake to cool in the tin for 10 mins, before turning out onto a wire rack to finish cooling. After 10 mins carefully transfer to the plate you would like the cake to be served on.
6 Serve with spoonfuls of Rodda's clotted cream and decorate with primrose flowers and extra granulated sugar.
RODDA'S

26 SUNDAY

27 MONDAY

28 TUESDAY

29 WEDNESDAY

30 THURSDAY

31 FRIDAY

1 SATURDAY

Precious memories

MY AMAZING BROTHER

This is a photo of me with my beloved brother Winston who was seven years younger than me. Our family's world fell apart when we were told he'd been in a road accident, aged twenty-two. Our immediate thought was that he had crashed his motorbike but it had happened while he was a passenger in a car.

The driver was dead and Winston was hanging on to life in hospital. He would never walk again. As he slowly recovered, he talked to the doctors and decided it was up to him to work hard, never giving in, although he would be in a wheelchair. He eventually returned home and all the family rallied round.

As the years passed there were lots of setbacks, but he never gave up. The doctors' prognosis of four years left to him was wrong. With dedication, determination and a love of life, he lived to be forty. He deserved a medal for endurance and the effort he put in to surviving this new, challenging life.

Sylvia Cummings, via email

Quick puzzle

Can you unscramble this 9-letter conundrum to form a word? You'll find the answer below.

MYRSDADAE

A: DAYDREAMS

Time for you

Nourish your body

90 per cent of your serotonin lies in your gut, so poor gut flora can affect your mood, appetite, sleep and memory. Incorporating gut-friendly foods in your daily diet such as natural yoghurt, walnuts and almonds, can help keep your mood up as well as keep any viruses at bay.

What a good idea!

Check your fridge temperature isn't too low or too high. To keep your food fresh and your fridge working efficiently, the temperature should be between 3°C and 5°C. Keeping your fridge around two thirds full will also help make it more energy efficient.

Box office blockbusters!

Michael Caine chose to wear glasses in The Ipcress File (1965) as he expected the film to be part of a franchise, so wanted to be able to remove them for other roles. When he broke three pairs while filming, production was held up for a day. An extra 20 pairs were then ordered.

Recipe of the week

MEXICAN BAKED EGGS IN TOMATOES

Serves: 4
Prep: 15 mins
Cook: 10 mins

1 tbsp oil
1 onion, finely sliced
1 red chilli, deseeded and finely chopped
1 tsp ground coriander
400g (14oz) can chopped tomatoes
4 medium eggs
1 ripe avocado, diced
2 tbsp roughly chopped coriander

1 Preheat the oven to 200°C/180°C Fan/Gas Mark 6.
2 Heat the oil in a large ovenproof frying pan and fry the onion and chilli for 4-5 mins until golden. Add the ground coriander and cook for a further minute.
3 Stir in the chopped tomatoes, season and cook for 1-2 mins. Make 4 hollows in the tomatoes and crack an egg into each. Bake for 8-9 mins until the egg whites have just set.
4 Sprinkle over the avocado and coriander to serve.
MILK & MORE

2 SUNDAY

PALM SUNDAY

3 MONDAY

4 TUESDAY

5 WEDNESDAY

6 THURSDAY

7 FRIDAY

GOOD FRIDAY

8 SATURDAY

Precious memories

AN ODE TO MY DAD

I wrote this poem in memory of my dear dad, William Henry Collins (Harry) who passed on in 2012.

He didn't change nappies and never did cook,
But he tinkered with cars
and stored nails in old jars.
He read to me stories, both old and new,
And taught me songs and rhymes that he knew.
He didn't play sports or go swimming with me,
Nor was he a drinker (except for coffee and tea).
Most of all, he never would shout or fight,
He was quiet and thoughtful
and knew what was right.
He designed tools in a factory for many a year,
Then worked in a college because it was near.
He played the church organ
from the age of eighteen
And the piano at home
on the weekdays between.
He took us for picnics with Mum by his side,
They were happy and blessed
going 'out for a ride'.
He recorded a diary and sent letters to friends,
He wrote books and made quizzes
– the list never ends.
He might have seemed serious,
but loved to laugh, too.
A dear friend and teacher
as well as the father I knew.
Christine J Blakeley, via email

Quick puzzle

Can you unscramble this 9-letter conundrum to form a word? You'll find the answer below.

TLROCOISI

A: SOLICITOR

Time for you

Join the **Yours** book club

Want to read more this year? Reduce stress and discover a variety of books while making new friends by joining a book club. For inspiration and discussion, why not join our friendly group? Find us at facebook.com/groups/yoursbookclub

What a good idea!

Kill established weeds with a solution of vinegar and salt. Mix one litre of white vinegar with three large spoons of both salt and washing up liquid. The salt and vinegar dry out the weeds, while the dish soap helps it stick.

Box office blockbusters!

Humphrey Bogart hated filming on location for The African Queen (1951) and complained about everything from the heat to the food. However, he was awarded with the only Oscar of his career. Katharine Hepburn was in her element in Africa but didn't win her Oscar.

Recipe of the week

EASTER LAMB

Serves: 6-8
Prep: 10 mins
Cook: 2 hours

2.3kg (5lbs) leg of lamb, bone in
Glug of olive oil
Sea salt & cracked black pepper
13g (½ oz) butter
2 onions, finely sliced
2 garlic cloves, chopped
1 tbsp balsamic vinegar
200ml (7 fl oz) white wine
2 sprigs fresh rosemary
Handful of parsley
1 lemon for the gravy
300ml (10 fl oz) lamb stock
2 sticks of celery and 3 carrots

1 Preheat the oven to 220°C/200°C Fan/Gas Mark 7. Use a basting brush to cover the joint lightly in olive oil and season. Roast the lamb in a large tray for 20 mins.
2 Heat the butter and a small glug of olive oil in a pan, add the sliced onions and fry until soft. Add the garlic and balsamic vinegar and let it simmer for a few mins. Pour in the wine and add 1 sprig of rosemary and some parsley. Simmer for a few mins more and then pour into the roasting tray around the lamb along with the lamb stock and celery/carrots.
3 Once the lamb has been cooking for 20 mins, turn the oven temperature down to 200°C/185°C Fan/Gas Mark 6, cover the joint with tin foil and roast until cooked. Roughly 20 mins per lb. Baste a few times throughout to ensure the meat is moist and flavourful.
4 Once the lamb reaches temperature, leave it to rest for around 30 mins before carving. Serve with the gravy and servings of your choice.
THERMAPEN

9 SUNDAY

EASTER SUNDAY

10 MONDAY

11 TUESDAY

12 WEDNESDAY

13 THURSDAY

14 FRIDAY

15 SATURDAY

Precious memories

HAPPY-GO-LUCKY SMILER

This is a photo of my mum and dad. Dad, who was known as The Smiler, was a bus driver based at Camberwell Green in south London. He was notorious for not sticking to the bus timetables. His early morning shifts took him to the West End where he picked up all the charladies from the hotels and offices, going off-route so the ladies didn't have to walk too far.

Some of the inspectors turned a blind eye to this, but not all of them did. There were many times when his clippie, Gladys, warned him that 'Old Blakey' was on the warpath so Dad would take an even bigger detour. His lady passengers were in fits of laughter and usually ended up having a sing song on the way home.

On Dad's weekends off we were all treated to breakfast in bed – boiled eggs with 'soldiers' and a cuppa. At Eastertime, he drew smiley faces on our boiled eggs before presenting us with the chocolate ones.

We four children are now in our 70s and we all have that happy-go-lucky attitude to life because Mum and Dad taught us to laugh, sing and dance through the rough times.
Pat Benton, Norfolk

Quick puzzle

Can you unscramble this 9-letter conundrum to form a word? You'll find the answer below.

IOGWRRNHA

A: HARROWING

Time for you

Buy yourself some flowers

It might be Easter, but if you fancy a change from chocolate, buy a bunch of flowers. It's a lovely pick-me-up – in fact, research conducted at Rutgers University confirms that they also make you more content, optimistic, and generally happier.

What a good idea!

How do you like your eggs at Easter? If the answer is hard boiled, try this clever trick for removing the shell easily. Fill a quarter of a glass jar with cold water. Place your boiled egg inside and tighten the lid. Shake vigorously until the shell slides off your egg. Enjoy!

Box office blockbusters!

After the success of the 1979 Alien film, Sigourney Weaver was initially reluctant to again take on the role of Ripley in Aliens (1986), until the impressive script changed her mind. Her resulting Best Actress nomination was the first ever for an actress in an action movie.

Recipe of the week

CARAMEL & GINGER HOT CROSS BUN BREAD & BUTTER PUDDING

Serves: 6
Prep: 20 mins
Cook: 35 mins

6 hot cross buns, sliced into 4
3 large eggs
300ml (10 fl oz) whipping cream
300ml (10 fl oz) milk
1 tsp vanilla extract
75g (3oz) golden caster sugar
3 balls of Opies Stem Ginger with Syrup, finely chopped, syrup reserved
3 tbsp Carnation caramel sauce
To serve:
Fresh warm custard
Some of the leftover caramel sauce

1 Take a large oven dish that will fit 6 hot cross buns comfortably and arrange the sliced hot cross buns in the dish.
2 In a large bowl whisk together the eggs, whipping cream, milk, vanilla extract, caster sugar and 2 tbsp of the reserved stem ginger syrup.
3 Pour the batter evenly over the hot cross buns. Scatter over the finely chopped stem ginger, cover and leave in the fridge for a couple of hours to allow the hot cross buns to absorb the mixture. You could also leave it overnight. Preheat the oven to 190°C / 170°C Fan/ Gas Mark 3.
4 Drizzle over half of the carnation caramel sauce and cook in the oven for about 30-35 mins, until the custard is set but still retaining a slight wobble.
5 Leave to cool slightly before serving with fresh custard and a little drizzle of caramel sauce.
OPIES

16 SUNDAY

17 MONDAY

18 TUESDAY

19 WEDNESDAY

20 THURSDAY

21 FRIDAY

22 SATURDAY

Precious memories

SWEET DEVON VIOLETS

I grew up in Dawlish, the home of Devon violet perfume so I associate the scent of violets with my childhood. In the heyday of the industry there were violet fields on the edge of town and a specially elected Violet Queen processed through the streets on a carnival float decorated with these flowers.

Many local shops stocked an enticing range of Devon violet gifts. There were soaps in porcelain dishes and painted pomanders containing petals mixed with other flowers. The perfume was often packaged in bottles with purple bows around their necks and the scent they contained was a surprisingly vivid shade of green. My favourite gift was a set of scented mauve notelets which I loved to use for writing thank-you letters.

Devon violets were a particular favourite of Queen Mary, the wife of George V. This made them a desirable fashion accessory in the Thirties. Bunches of freshly picked violets were transported to London daily by train to Covent Garden from where they were sold by flower girls around the city.

When Princess Elizabeth married Prince Philip in 1947, Dawlish town council presented the happy couple with Devon violets displayed in a pottery bowl.
Susannah White, via email

Quick puzzle

Can you unscramble this 9-letter conundrum to form a word? You'll find the answer below.

NEWVERTII

A: INTERVIEW

Time for you

Try a power pose

If you're lacking in confidence, give yourself a boost with power posing. A good one to try for two minutes every day, or before you do something that worries you, is the 'Wonder Woman' pose with your feet wide, chest out and hands on hips.

What a good idea!

Store your plastic bags more tidily in an empty tissue box. Push your first bag into the box so just the two handles are poking out, then pass the body of the next bag through the handles and push this bag into the box. Repeat until your box is full.

Box office blockbusters!

The all-star cast of The Magnificent Seven (1960) were a competitive lot, particularly when it came to screen time. Yul Brynner would stand on mounds of earth to make himself look taller while Steve McQueen would play with his hat during Yul's scene to get attention.

Recipe of the week

RHUBARB COMPOTE

Serves: 8
Prep: 5 mins
Cook: 45 mins

1kg (2lb) rhubarb zest
Juice of 2 oranges
1 vanilla pod split length ways
125g (4oz) caster sugar

1 Preheat the oven to 120°C/100°C Fan/Gas Mark ½. Wash the rhubarb and cut into uniformly sized pieces and arrange in a baking dish.
2 Sprinkle the orange zest and juice, the vanilla pod and the sugar over the rhubarb.
3 Gently cook in the oven for 45 mins until the rhubarb is tender but still holding its shape. Allow to cool before serving. This compote will last up to 2 weeks in the fridge or 6 months in the freezer.

RODDA'S

23 SUNDAY

ST GEORGES DAY

24 MONDAY

25 TUESDAY

26 WEDNESDAY

27 THURSDAY

28 FRIDAY

29 SATURDAY

Precious memories

A TOY STORY

Here is a photo of me with some of my toys. I still have my teddy bear. His name is John and he is eighty-nine years old. He is in a very dilapidated state and he has no eyes. Apparently my mother removed them because they were fixed with metal pins which could have been pulled out quite easily by a child.

During the war, my sister Jill and I gathered together all our dolls and teddies and started a school for them in our empty garage. Being the older one, I was the headmistress, Miss Jones, and my sister was Mrs Smith. We measured the dolls and teddies and divided them into two classes according to height. John was head of the junior school. He was a very clever pupil!

John and I have been through so much together. He was a great comfort to me when we had to sleep in the Morrison shelter during air raids. He still sits in my bedroom. (Incidentally, my husband's name was John, too!)
Nanette Mereweather

Quick puzzle

Can you unscramble this 9-letter conundrum to form a word? You'll find the answer below.

EIASENXTI

A: ANXIETIES

Time for you

Write down some positive affirmations

We can all do with a pick-me-up and some positivity to keep the blues at bay. Kind words can be powerful, whether these are to ourselves, or those spoken by others. Read your positive affirmations whenever you're having a tough day and write down more regularly to help reinforce the positivity in your own mind.

What a good idea!

Try this if you find ironing sheets a chore. Make your bed with your freshly washed sheets. Fill an empty spray bottle with a capful of fabric softener and water. Spritz lightly over your bedding stretching it out tightly. Leave to dry and they'll be crease free and smell gorgeous.

Box office blockbusters!

Al Pacino refused to attend the Oscars when he was nominated for Best Actor in a Supporting Role for his part as Michael in The Godfather (1972) – arguing he had more screen time than co-star Brando, who was nominated for (and won) Best Actor.

Recipe of the week

THAI GREEN CURRY

Serves: 4
Prep: 10 mins
Cook: 25 mins

2 tbsp sesame oil
3 tbsp Thai green curry paste
2 cm piece fresh ginger, grated
3 spring onions, finely chopped
1 long red chilli, deseeded and finely chopped (optional)
2 tbsp tamari
1 tsp coconut sugar
10-12 florets tenderstem broccoli
(or 1 small head broccoli)
395ml (14fl oz) light coconut milk
85g (3oz) snow peas
32g (1oz) roughly chopped fresh coriander
32g (1oz) basil
1 pack Fry's Vegan Chicken-style Strips or 300g plant-based chicken
1 tsp sesame oil
2 tbsp maple syrup
2 tbsp sesame seeds

1 In a large pan heat the sesame oil over a medium-high heat. Add the curry paste, ginger, spring onions and chilli, then sauté for approximately 2 mins or until fragrant.
2 Add the tamari, coconut sugar, broccoli, coconut milk and peas. Bring to a simmer over a low heat and cook for 10-12 mins.
3 Add the coriander and basil in the last 5 mins of cooking and stir through thoroughly.
4 In a separate pan, lightly fry the vegan strips or tofu in the sesame oil until warmed through (approx 6 mins). Add the maple syrup and allow to caramelise over the strips or tofu.
5 Remove from the heat and sprinkle over the sesame seeds.
6 Serve with basmati or jasmine rice.
FRY FAMILY FOOD CO

30 SUNDAY

1 MONDAY

2 TUESDAY

3 WEDNESDAY

4 THURSDAY

5 FRIDAY

6 SATURDAY

Precious memories

HERE COMES THE BRIDE

Here I am on my wedding day in 1967 with my dad, Dave. We lived in the village of Woodside where he was the local publican. The year before my wedding he had suffered a mild stroke so he walked with a limp.

I remember that car journey to the church so well. I was proud to be sitting with Dad who was always kind and thoughtful to everyone. As we drove along the twisting country lane he asked the chauffeur to stop for a minute so that an old lady we knew could see us in our wedding finery.

My husband-to-be came from a large family and many of our pub regulars were there so the church was filled to the brim and the hymns were sung with great gusto. I remember feeling butterflies in my stomach as we walked up the aisle. Dad was his usual calm self.

After the service, my auntie pulled me to one side and told me to be 'more careful' than she had been as her first baby had been born exactly nine months after her wedding. Our first son was born nearly two years later so we had been more careful than auntie!

Linda Hurdwell, via email

Quick puzzle

Can you unscramble this 9-letter conundrum to form a word? You'll find the answer below.

FODATRRVE

A: OVERDRAFT

Time for you

Banish anxiety

Sometimes, just counting back from 100 in threes is a good way to stop yourself from overthinking and to shut the door on a negative cycle of thoughts. After all, it's tricky to count back from 100 in threes and think about anything else at the same time!

What a good idea!

Remove scorch marks on your iron with this simple method using just an uncoated paracetamol tablet. Wear oven gloves to protect your hands and turn your iron onto the highest setting. Using tweezers gently rub the tablet over the marked areas and wipe away the dirt with a cloth.

Box office blockbusters!

James Dean was so immersed in his character in Giant (1956) that he rarely changed out of his costume, but for Elizabeth Taylor and Rock Hudson the film was the start of a lifelong friendship. They struggled filming their wedding scene after partying the night before!

Recipe of the week

ASPARAGUS & SORREL PUFF PASTRY TART

Serves: 8
Prep: 5 mins
Cook: 25 mins

500g (1lb) British asparagus (medium-fine spears)
50g (2oz) sorrel leaves
200ml (7oz) full-fat crème fraîche
25g (1oz) parmesan, finely grated
1tbsp light olive oil
320g (11oz) ready-rolled all butter puff pastry sheet

1 Preheat the oven to 200°C/180°C Fan/Gas Mark 6. Place a wide saucepan on to boil. Meanwhile, snap the woody ends from the asparagus, discard those ends and set the spears to one side.
2 Chop three-quarters of the sorrel leaves finely. Add the crème fraîche into a bowl and stir the chopped sorrel and parmesan through it. Add the asparagus spears to boiling water and blanch them for 30 secs. Drain through a sieve, chill completely under running cold water, then leave to dry for 1-2 mins.
3 Roll the asparagus in the olive oil so each is glossy. Unroll the pastry sheet. Put a sheet of baking parchment on a large baking tray. Lay the pastry on top, and score a border 3cm from the edge using the blunt edge of a knife. Spread the crème fraîche and sorrel paste on top, right up to the edges. Arrange the asparagus spears across the middle.
4 Bake in the oven for 20-25 mins. Allow to cool for 5 mins, then finely shred the remaining sorrel and sprinkle over the top.
ED SMITH

7 SUNDAY

8 MONDAY

9 TUESDAY

10 WEDNESDAY

11 THURSDAY

12 FRIDAY

13 SATURDAY

Precious memories

A TROUBLED CHILDHOOD

I was born in 1949 and my parents, Doris and George, were devout Roman Catholics who lived in a large house in a London suburb. Although I had plenty of toys and outings I often felt lonely as there weren't many other children in the neighbourhood. I would have loved to have a brother or sister.

My father was a quiet, easygoing man who at times disagreed with decisions about my strict upbringing. Sometimes at night I would hear shouting from downstairs which frightened me. My mother said it was just the radio, but as I got older I realised it was my parents arguing. When I was five, they separated.

Aged seventeen, I was planning a trip to Ireland to meet a friend. As I started to complete the passport application form, my mother put her arms around me and started crying. She then explained that I had been adopted.

I resented my birth mother for giving me up and after my adoptive mother died I struggled emotionally and with practical issues, but now I live a fulfilling life with wonderful friends and a close family and understand the reasons my birth mother was unable to keep me. After many years of searching, I have been unable to trace her.

Ann Martin, via email

Quick puzzle

Can you unscramble this 9-letter conundrum to form a word? You'll find the answer below.

LADEYMSHA

A: ASHAMEDLY

Time for you

Head outside

It's vital to spend some time outside each day, even if it's just a quick walk around the block, your local high street or local park. Walking has been proven effective in reducing anxiety and depression, and there is further evidence that walking in nature improves those results even further.

What a good idea!

Use a baker's muffin tin to perfectly space out seeds when planting. Weed and prepare the soil of your planting area. Then push the tin into the soil, so the muffin sections create evenly spaced planting holes. Drop your seeds into the holes, cover and water.

Box office blockbusters!

The epic Lawrence of Arabia (1962) took longer to make than it did for the real T.E. Lawrence to go from Lieutenant to Colonel and to see the desert tribes united. It's also, at 3 hours and 36 minutes, the longest movie not to have any dialogue spoken by a woman.

Recipe of the week

LAMB BIRYANI

Serves: 3-4
Prep: 8 mins
Cook:15 mins

2 tbsp vegetable oil
2 onions, sliced
Salt and ground black pepper
5 medium British Lion eggs
2cm piece root ginger, grated
1 clove garlic, crushed
3 tbsp medium curry paste
175g-225g (6-8oz) cold roast lamb, beef, chicken or turkey
225g (8oz) cooked vegetables (we used cauliflower, broccoli and peas)
200g (7oz) sachet of cooked basmati rice
3 tbsp chopped fresh coriander
50g (2oz) pomegranate seeds

1 Heat the oil in a large frying pan or wok. Add the onions and a pinch of salt, then cook over a medium heat for 6-8 mins, until onions are brown.
2 Remove half the onions and set aside. Cook the remainder over a low heat until golden and crispy. Drain on kitchen paper.
3 While you cook the onions, place the eggs in a small pan, cover with cold water and bring to the boil and cook for 5 mins. Drain the eggs, rinse in cold water, tapping the shells all over. When cool enough to handle, peel away the shells and set aside.
4 Return the soft onions to the pan with the ginger, garlic and curry paste and cook over a medium heat, stirring for a few secs. Add the roasted meat, vegetables and rice with 4 tbsp water.
5 Continue to cook, stirring frequently to mix everything together until all the ingredients are piping hot. Stir in half the coriander and season to taste.
6 Transfer to a serving platter topped with the crispy fried onions, remaining coriander and pomegranate seeds. Cut the eggs in half and place on top. They should still be slightly soft inside.
BRITISH LION EGGS

14 SUNDAY

15 MONDAY

16 TUESDAY

17 WEDNESDAY

18 THURSDAY

19 FRIDAY

20 SATURDAY

Precious memories

THE SOUND OF MUSIC

This is my mother, Eva Selby. The photo was taken when she was eighty-three and had just been honoured with a special long service certificate from the Methodist Music Society for having been an organist for seventy-one years. The award came as a complete surprise to her and she was quite overwhelmed.

When she was twelve years old she started playing the harmonium in her parents' home. When she found she enjoyed it, she had lessons. She went on to play for the junior church, then the Sunday School and eventually the chapel services. Remarkably, she was still a teenager when she played at her tutor's wedding ceremony.

When the electronic organ became popular she and my father took lessons and found this quite a new experience after pedalling for all those years. They used to meet up with friends for evenings of organ music in each other's homes and had some lovely times.

She was a wonderful mother to my brother and me and gave so much enjoyment to other people through her music. Sadly, she died in 2001 at the age of ninety, but happy memories last forever.

Margaret Carter, Purton

Quick puzzle

Can you unscramble this 9-letter conundrum to form a word? You'll find the answer below.

TEEUARCRS

A: CREATURES

Time for you

Start with a song

Research shows setting your favourite song as an alarm to wake you up could be the best way to start your day on the right foot. The researchers found a melodic alarm that you can sing along to, as opposed to the traditional dreaded 'beep-beep' can in fact boost alertness throughout the day.

What a good idea!

Use olive oil to restore your wooden chopping boards and utensils. Apply a light coat, let it soak for a few minutes and then buff any leftover oil into the wood for a healthy shine. It also makes a great furniture polish too, as it helps repel water from spillages.

Box office blockbusters!

The trash compactor scene in Star Wars (1977) took its toll – Mark Hamill (Luke Skywalker) broke a blood vessel in his face after holding his breath so long during filming the scene. Meanwhile, the Chewbacca suit worn retained a bad smell after filming it...

Recipe of the week

WILD GARLIC & NEW POTATO FRITTATA

Serves: 4
Prep: 5 mins
Cook: 20 mins

200g (7oz) small new potatoes
8 large eggs
20-25 wild garlic leaves, roughly chopped
100g (4oz) podded fresh peas (optional)
80g (3oz) soft goat's cheese, such as a Perroche
30g (1oz) butter

1 Place the potatoes in a saucepan of cold water. Place over a medium-high heat. Boil then simmer for 8-12 mins, until the potatoes are tender. Drain, then leave under a running cold tap until room temperature or less. Slice in half lengthways.
2 Break the eggs into a large mixing bowl. Whisk thoroughly and season. Add the potatoes and the peas (if using). Turn your grill on. Place a non-stick, heavy bottomed frying pan on a medium heat. Add a knob of butter. When that's melted, add the wild garlic and allow to wilt for 1 min.
3 Turn the heat up and add the rest of the butter. After 15-20 secs, the butter should be frothing. Pour in the egg mixture and push the potatoes around so they're evenly spaced. Turn the heat down a little and cook the frittata for 4 mins. Dot chunks of goat's cheese around the frittata, then place the pan about under the grill.
4 Cook for 2-3 mins. Remove and leave to rest and firm up for 5-10 mins, then slip the frittata out of the pan onto a serving plate.

ED SMITH

21 SUNDAY

22 MONDAY

23 TUESDAY

24 WEDNESDAY

25 THURSDAY

26 FRIDAY

27 SATURDAY

Precious memories

FIRST LOVE, TRUE LOVE

When I was thirteen I saw a wedding dress in a shop window in London and said to my mum and sister that it was the dress I would like when I got married.

When I was fourteen I came home from school to find my blind date waiting on his scooter. Unsure of my feelings, I just said: "Hello". He asked me on a date to the circus on the Rye at High Wycombe. I went on the bus to meet him there. He was worried that I would think him too fast if he asked to hold my hand.

Mum and I were eavesdropping when Brian asked my dad if he could marry me. Dad gave his consent and we got engaged when I was sixteen. We bought my engagement ring from Ratner's (it cost £25) before going to the cinema to see South Pacific.

As Brian's auntie was moving to Australia, we had the opportunity to buy her three-bedroomed house and moved in a week after my eighteenth birthday in February 1966. I bought my wedding dress from the shop in London and my sister said I looked like a princess.

We have been blessed with two wonderful children and four grandchildren.
Sally Phillips, High Wycombe

Quick puzzle

Can you unscramble this 9-letter conundrum to form a word? You'll find the answer below.

TIFFEROID

A: FORTIFIED

Time for you

Give back

If you enjoy giving back to others (and it is possible for this to extend beyond your family!), consider what you can do in your local area to spread the love. It could just be volunteering or fundraising for a charity close to your heart.

What a good idea!

How often do you clean your mattress? Vacuuming yours every month will help keep dust mites at bay and can help reduce allergies triggered by dust. Freshen yours up by applying a thin layer of baking soda over the mattress surface. Leave for a few hours before vacuuming thoroughly.

Box office blockbusters!

Alec Guinness initially turned down the role of Colonel Nicholson in The Bridge on the River Kwai (1957), saying, "I can't imagine anyone wanting to watch a stiff-upper-lip British Colonel for two-and-a half hours." They did, and he went on to win his only Oscar.

Recipe of the week

PEACH AND RASPBERRY FRANGIPANE TART

Serves: 8
Prep: 10 mins
Cook: 40 mins

375g (13oz) ready rolled shortcrust pastry sheet
175g (6oz) butter, softened
175g (6oz) caster sugar
175g (6oz) ground almonds
4 eggs
5 tbsp raspberry jam
1 jar Opies Peaches with Courvoisier®, syrup reserved
30g (1oz) raspberries
2 tbsp flaked almonds
To serve:
Icing sugar, for dusting
300ml (11fl oz) double cream

1 Preheat the oven to 180°C/ 160°C Fan/ Gas Mark 4.
2 Drape the pastry sheet over a large shallow flan dish and prick the base with a fork. Trim the edges and set aside.
3 Add the butter and sugar to a food processor and whizz until pale and creamy. Next add the ground almonds and process again until combined. Finally add the eggs and 3 tbsp of reserved syrup, pulsing again until soft and creamy.
4 Spread a layer of raspberry jam over the base of the pastry then spoon the almond mixture on top. Place the peach halves on top (cut side down) and press them down lightly, before dotting any gaps with raspberries, making sure they are pushed into the mixture.
5 Scatter with the flaked almonds then bake in the oven for 35-40 mins or until set and golden.
6 Dust with icing sugar and serve warm or cold with some cream.
OPIES

28 SUNDAY

29 MONDAY

30 TUESDAY

31 WEDNESDAY

1 THURSDAY

2 FRIDAY

3 SATURDAY

Precious memories

DANCING GIRLS

When I was auditioning for a pantomime in 1978, I was asked if I would like to be a dancer in Istanbul instead. Initially, I said no, but it was an Equity contract and I would be able to get my full card. (Equity cards were very hard to get back then.) Plus I was offered a fabulous salary and wonderful dance routines.

A month later I couldn't believe I was on that plane to Turkey where I was met by three other British girls. Together we shared a tiny dressing-room as well as memorable experiences such as visiting Taksim Square and eating mussel soup in a café by the Bosphorus Bridge. I remember being fascinated by the unfamiliar fruit and vegetables sold from a stall – we had nothing like them in England at that time. We also became adept at learning Turkish. I still know a lot of words now.

Living abroad makes you grow as a person and I'll never forget my six months in that glamorous, absorbing city and the friends that I made. The four of us met up recently and, despite the venue being St Pancras station, we were transported back to those wonderful days in Istanbul.
Heather Moulson, via email

Quick puzzle
Can you unscramble this 9-letter conundrum to form a word? You'll find the answer below.

YPARTDIVE

A: DEPRAVITY

Time for you

Drink water

It's one we can all do with a reminder of, but drinking water can have some amazing benefits for your physical and mental wellbeing including your immune system, mood, memory and energy. Be sure to drink 8-10 glasses of water a day to keep your brain nourished and body flushed of toxins.

What a good idea!

Essential oils can make great household air fresheners. Add a few drops of your favourites to balls of cotton wool and hide around your home. Also, pop a scented ball in your vacuum cleaner too and the smell will fill your home whenever you vacuum.

Box office blockbusters!

More than 80 make-up artists were involved in Planet of the Apes (1968) – no wonder then that this movie holds the record for highest make-up budget (when adjusted for inflation). At $345,542, the make-up bill made up about 17 per cent of the film's total budget!

Recipe of the week

KOREAN BIBIMBAP GUKSU BOWL

Serves: 1
Prep: 15 mins
Cook: 10 mins

1 tbsp cooking oil
100g (4oz) minced beef
1 tbsp Sun Hee Gochujang
1 tbsp mirin and a little salt
2 tbsp Sun Hee Doenjang
2 tbsp light soy sauce
Cold water
200g (7oz) boiled rice noodles
½ carrot, julienne
4 spring onions, sliced lengthways
Handful of bean sprouts
70g (2oz) sautéed mushrooms
Handful of green beans
1 egg
Sesame seeds to sprinkle
Sun Hee Kimchi fermented cabbage

1 Add the oil to a medium hot pan before adding the minced beef, Sun Hee Gochujang paste, mirin and salt to taste. Cook for 2 mins then sprinkle over some water. Cover and cook for another 7-8 mins. Set aside once cooked.
2 To make the sauce, in a medium hot saucepan add the Sun Hee Doenjang paste, light soy sauce and 2 tbsp of water. Mix together well until runny and set aside for later.
3 To assemble the bowl, add the cooked rice noodles at the centre and add the vegetables and cooked beef mince around them. Fry the egg and place it in the centre, on top of the noodles. Serve hot with the sauce you made earlier, and sprinkle with sesame seeds. Serve with Sun Hee Kimchi fermented cabbage.
SUN HEE

4 SUNDAY

5 MONDAY

6 TUESDAY

7 WEDNESDAY

8 THURSDAY

9 FRIDAY

10 SATURDAY

Precious memories

A DORSET PAGEANT

In the summer of 1953 many members of my family took part in a pageant to celebrate the anniversary of Bridport receiving a Royal charter. My grandfather, Vernon Payne, opened the proceedings dressed as Old Father Time. He wore a white wig and flowing beard and carried a scythe.

My grandmother played an Elizabethan courtier while my mother and her brother were page boys dressed in doublet and hose and red velvet cloaks. They practised dancing the pavane in the municipal gardens behind the council offices and my mother felt joyful, cycling through the town with her red cloak billowing behind her.

A family friend was in the Ancient Britain scene. As he was driving along, dressed in his furry caveman outfit, he spotted an accident – a cyclist had fallen into a ditch. The young man was not badly hurt, but he had a terrible shock when he opened his eyes to see an Ancient Briton bending over him!

Large stands were built on the playing fields for the audience and there was great excitement when Princess Margaret opened the show. My grandparents attended a reception for her at the town hall where a new toilet was installed especially for her use.
Susie Myers, via email

Quick puzzle
Can you unscramble this 9-letter conundrum to form a word? You'll find the answer below.

BASECLAN

A: BALANCES

Time for you

Download the Couch to 5k app

This easy-to-follow programme will start you off running for eight minutes (with plenty of breaks), gradually working up to a 5k run in as little as nine weeks. You can also connect with like-minded people through the Couch to 5k forum, which is full of advice, tips and motivation.

What a good idea!

While most of us love the smell of fresh oranges, pests and aphids definitely do not, so it makes a great natural deterrent. Add orange peel to a spray bottle along with some hot water. Shake and allow to cool before spraying on any plants at risk!

Box office blockbusters!

Filming Roman Holiday (1953) was a joy for Audrey Hepburn, in her break-out starring role. On its release, the film was a huge hit, Hepburn was a sensation and when she won her Oscar, she was so overwhelmed she left it in the ladies' toilets!

Recipe of the week

APPLE COURGETTI SALAD WITH A TAHINI DRESSING

Serves: 1
Prep: 5 mins
Cook: 3 mins

For the tahini dressing:
2 tbsp of tahini
The juice of ½ lemon
½ tsp of white miso paste
½ tsp of maple syrup
1 tsp of apple cider vinegar
For the rest:
Water to thin as desired
3 tbsp walnuts roughly chopped
1 JAZZ™Apple
1 courgette
A generous handful of rocket
Salt and pepper to taste

1 To make the tahini dressing simply mix together all the ingredients. Use a small whisk to avoid any lumps. Add the water gradually until it's the right consistency.
2 Toast the chopped walnuts in a frying pan on a medium heat for a few mins, tossing them from time to time until they start to turn golden brown.
3 Spiralize the apple and the courgette. Transfer them to a large bowl and pour over the tahini dressing. Mix in the rocket. Serve straight away with the toasted walnuts.
JAZZ™ APPLE

11 SUNDAY

12 MONDAY

13 TUESDAY

14 WEDNESDAY

15 THURSDAY

16 FRIDAY

17 SATURDAY

Precious memories

UNDER AN AFRICAN SUN

Here I am with my cat, Dusty, who travelled with us when we moved to Rhodesia (now Zimbabwe) in 1968. My father was employed by British Oxygen and he saw this as an ideal opportunity for a better life for our family.

It was a huge cultural difference with servants to cook and clean for us. The climate was also a big change with very high temperatures and bright blue skies day after day. We lived in a bungalow with a large garden. The bungalows were widely spaced out to prevent the spread of flames in the event of a bush fire.

Aged sixteen, I found it very difficult to settle as there was little to do apart from a two-mile walk in the heat to the local shops.

Sadly, we returned home sooner than anticipated which was a shame as I was just beginning to get used to the different way of life. However, I do have some happy memories of some exciting journeys, driving through the bush and seeing wild animals in their natural habitat. I have never returned, but it was an experience that will never be forgotten.
Philippa Herrington, via email

Quick puzzle

Can you unscramble this 9-letter conundrum to form a word? You'll find the answer below.

IANTINGLE

A: ENTAILING

Time for you

Do nothing

The world is a busy place and it's easy to get caught up in the idea that we should be doing something at all times. Whenever you get moments of quiet, don't be afraid to revel in the nothingness and enjoy the peace and tranquillity it can bring to your mind and body.

What a good idea!

For streak-free bathroom mirrors, swap your fancy glass cleaner for this bathroom essential. Apply a squirt of shaving foam directly to the surface before buffing it in with a microfiber cloth. It's great for making glass sparkle, but also prevents mirrors steaming up during a bath or shower!

Box office blockbusters!

Mia Farrow was hired for Rosemary's Baby (1968) on the strength of her TV work for Peyton Place. While filming, her husband Frank Sinatra (who was 29 years her senior) served her divorce papers. Her marriage ended but the film made Farrow an established film star.

Recipe of the week

BARBECUE KEBABS

Serves: 4
Prep: 25 mins
Cook: 5 mins

1 x 340g (12oz) can of SPAM® Chopped Pork and Ham cut into 1in cubes
1 x red pepper – cut into 1in cubes
1 x yellow pepper – cut into 1in cubes
large red onion – cut into quarters and each quarter halved horizontally to give 8 pieces/chunks
8 x chestnut mushrooms
vegetable oil for brushing
1 x small jar mango chutney (optional)
kebab sticks – previously been soaked in water

1 Thread cubes of SPAM® Chopped Pork and Ham on to soaked kebab sticks alternating with the vegetables to give a colourful portion.
2 Brush the kebabs with oil and a little mango chutney if using and place on the hot barbecue, turning them over until all the SPAM® Chopped Pork and Ham and vegetables are nicely browned all over and cooked.

SPAM

18 SUNDAY

19 MONDAY

20 TUESDAY

21 WEDNESDAY

22 THURSDAY

23 FRIDAY

24 SATURDAY

Precious memories

MY FIRST SWEETHEART

It was at a funfair in my home town that I met my first sweetheart. His name was Dave and he was down from London for the day with his mate, Mike. I was with my friend Joy who got chatting to Mike.

Dave and I went for a walk to an espresso coffee bar. We shyly held hands. Our first kiss stirred up feelings I'd never experienced before. Although we were both sixteen Dave was still at a public school and I was a working girl.

We corresponded during the following weeks until he and Mike came to visit us once more. We walked the four miles to Joy's house and I can still remember Chris Barber's Petite Fleur playing as we passed a record shop. As long as we were together we were happy.

Dave and I continued to correspond. His last letter told me he was in hospital with a lump on his knee. I did not appreciate how serious it was. After all, we were young and infallible. I heard no more until a letter arrived from his sister to say that Dave had passed away. I was shocked and dumbfounded. Our romance was cut short but he will always be my first love.
Irene Rogers, via email

Quick puzzle

Can you unscramble this 9-letter conundrum to form a word? You'll find the answer below.

RHINETIDE

A: INHERITED

Time for you

Try something new

Engaging in a new activity can help keep things fresh in your mind as well as help you find new enjoyable things to unlock. You could try a new hobby or start small by taking a new route on your daily walk. Or why not take part in our 50 over 50 challenge?

What a good idea!

Keep your houseplants happy with this self-watering system. Place a water-filled container on a raised surface above your plants. Tie a paperclip to a piece of cotton string and place at the bottom of the water container. Take the other end of string and push into the soil of each pot.

Box office blockbusters!

After audiences saw Elliott lure ET out of hiding using Reese's Pieces in 1982 sales of the chocolate shot up by 65 per cent in two weeks. Hershey's paid $1 million to provide product placement for the blockbuster and it paved the way for product placement in film.

Recipe of the week

VEGAN SUMMER PASTA

Serves: 2
Prep: 10 mins
Cook: 20 mins

200g (7oz) pasta of your choice
4 tsp extra-virgin olive oil
1 medium courgette (cut into chunks)
2 garlic cloves (roughly chopped)
2 large ripe tomatoes (chopped)
8 cherry tomatoes (halved)
2 tsp balsamic vinegar
Pinch of chilli flakes
8 Kalamata olives (de-stoned and chopped)
Salt and black pepper for seasoning
1 tsp Bioglan Superfoods Supergreens
Fresh parsley to garnish (optional)

1 Start cooking your pasta of choice following the instructions on the packet.
2 Meanwhile, heat 2 tsp of oil in a pan and once hot add the courgette. Fry gently until caramelised.
3 Once the courgette is caramelised add the chopped garlic and stir constantly to make sure the garlic doesn't brown. Season the mixture and fry for about 2-3 mins and then transfer out of the pan and set aside.
4 Add a dash of water to the pan you used for the courgette and then add the chopped tomatoes. Allow time for the tomatoes to break down and the sauce to thicken. Then add the cherry tomatoes and wait for them to soften in the sauce.
5 Season the sauce and add the balsamic vinegar as well as some chilli flakes.
6 Once the pasta is cooked, drain and add to the tomato sauce, mixing well.
7 Return the courgette and garlic back to the pan and mix with the pasta and sauce, adding the olives too.
8 Serve in bowls, sprinkle the Supergreens over the top and add fresh parsley to garnish.
BIOGLAN

25 SUNDAY

26 MONDAY

27 TUESDAY

28 WEDNESDAY

29 THURSDAY

30 FRIDAY

1 SATURDAY

Precious memories

GONE FISHING WITH DAD

I was one of four children and the only girl. My mother told me that she and my father moved to the village of Langold so that Dad could get work in the coal mine and a house to live in.

I loved my dad and I often think of the happy times the two of us shared; the endless days sat on a river bank fishing or hours spent weeding on his allotment. When he was working shifts he relied on me to water and feed the pigs he kept there and to check on his plants. A local butcher would come and take one of the pigs and return it to us cut up into joints and sides of bacon. The dripping spread on toast was delicious.

One memory I have of my dad is going with him on his motorbike to the dentist to have all his teeth taken out. I don't think anaesthetic was used but, job done, we got back on the bike and came home. Before that occasion, he had pulled the odd ones out himself using pliers.

This photo of him was taken when he had just arrived home from a day out fishing in Bridlington.

Alma Bonser, Worksop

Quick puzzle

Can you unscramble this 9-letter conundrum to form a word? You'll find the answer below.

GLUEDIVAN

A: DEVALUING

Time for you

Stretch out

Yoga can help you focus on your body and discover how you're feeling. Sure, it's not going to be the same as a full yoga class, but 15 seconds in downward dog, stretching out your hips and really feeling your body, can work wonders.

What a good idea!

If you love strawberries as much as you love Wimbledon, make yours last longer with this clever trick. Mix ¼ cup of white vinegar with 1 ½ cup water. Add the strawberries and soak for two minutes. Drain and dry and they'll stay fresh for up to two weeks.

Box office blockbusters!

MGM's epic Ben-Hur (1959) cost $15 million to make. The chariot race alone required 15,000 extras and took five weeks to film. Despite the outlay, it made a huge profit (earning $75m) and was the first film to win 11 Academy Awards.

Recipe of the week

PANNA COTTA

Serves: 8
Prep: 15 mins
Cook: 5 mins

2½ sheets of gelatine, soaked
700g (1½lb) Rodda's Cornish clotted cream
250ml (9 fl oz) Rodda's Cornish milk
1 vanilla pod (bean), split
150g (5oz) icing sugar, sifted

1 Immerse the gelatine in a small bowl of cold water and leave to soak. Add half of the clotted cream, all of the milk and the split vanilla pod into a heavy-based pan and slowly bring to just under a simmer. Do not boil the water, just warm enough to allow the gelatine to dissolve in the clotted cream.
2 Remove from the heat and leave to infuse for 10 mins. In a separate bowl, combine the remaining clotted cream with the icing sugar. Return the infused clotted cream mixture to the heat to warm through.
3 Remove the gelatine from the water, squeezing out any excess liquid, then add to the warmed clotted cream and stir to dissolve. Pour the infused mixture through a fine sieve onto the cold clotted cream and icing sugar and stir well. Pour into small espresso mugs, then chill in the refrigerator for at least 3 hours or overnight.

RODDA'S

2 SUNDAY

3 MONDAY

4 TUESDAY

5 WEDNESDAY

6 THURSDAY

7 FRIDAY

8 SATURDAY

Precious memories

LIFE IN SINGAPORE

My first experience of living in another country was in 1965 when my husband, who was in the RAF, was posted to Singapore.

I had never flown before so it was quite daunting as we were travelling with our four small children in a noisy turbo prop plane. The journey took 28 hours with a couple of short stops for refuelling. There was some turbulence which was a bit scary, but the children accepted it all without complaint.

On arrival of course the climate hit us – it was so humid! But after a week or two we got acclimatised and really enjoyed the heat. We were provided with an amah who took over the general running of the house. That took a bit of getting used to, but it was very nice. Another world, really!

In the three years that we lived in Singapore we were able to explore the island and visit many temples as well as other places of historical interest. The photo shows the Olympic-sized swimming pool at RAF Seletar where, as a family, we spent many happy hours. My children learned to swim like fish at a very early age.

Jill Cailes, via email

Quick puzzle

Can you unscramble this 9-letter conundrum to form a word? You'll find the answer below.

NICKINEGS

A: SICKENING

Time for you

Notice five things

Next time you're on a walk, tune in to your surroundings by noticing five interesting things that you can see, hear, feel, or smell. This simple exercise invites you to notice what is new, unique, or things that you may not have paid attention to before.

What a good idea!

If you haven't got round to finishing off that bottle of wine from last week, don't be tempted to pour it away. Freeze it instead! Add to an ice-cube tray and you'll have perfectly sized portions for risotto and other dishes when needed.

Box office blockbusters!

Jaws (1975) was originally supposed to be released in time for Christmas 1974 but because filming overran, it was pushed back to summer – the worst time for movies to be released in America. When 67 million people in the US went to see it, it became the first summer blockbuster.

Recipe of the week

HASSELBACK SQUASH WITH WALNUT CRUMB

Serves: 2
Prep: 15 mins
Cook: 1 hour

1 butternut squash, peeled, halved and deseeded (1.3kg)
2 cloves garlic, sliced
3 tbsp olive oil, plus a drizzle
2 tsp ground cumin
1 tsp ground coriander
75g (3oz) California Walnuts, chopped, plus 25g (1oz)
½ x 25g (1oz) pack fresh coriander, chopped, plus extra to serve
2 tbsp chopped chives
1 lemon
150g (5oz) edamame beans

1 Preheat the oven to 200°C/180°C Fan/ Gas Mark 6. Place 1 squash half, flat side down on a chopping board between 2 wooden spoons (to stop the knife cutting all the way through). Make cuts, ½ cm apart all the way along the squash. Repeat with the other squash half and place both in a roasting tin, push the garlic slices randomly into the cuts.
2 Mix 2 tbsp oil with the spices and drizzle over the squash, bake for 40 mins.
3 Mix the 75g (3oz) walnuts, herbs, lemon zest and remaining oil together and sprinkle over the squash, bake for a further 20 mins until golden and tender.
4 Meanwhile, stir fry the beans and remaining 25g (1oz) walnuts in a drizzle of oil for 1-2 mins, stirring in the juice of half the lemon at the end. Serve with the squash.

CALIFORNIA WALNUTS

9 SUNDAY

10 MONDAY

11 TUESDAY

12 WEDNESDAY

13 THURSDAY

14 FRIDAY

15 SATURDAY

Precious memories

HOLIDAYS AFLOAT

We spent many happy hours cruising the waterways of England and Wales in our traditional seventy-foot narrowboat called Venus which we had converted to sleep ten people. Our permanent mooring was Saul Junction from where a trip up the Gloucester Sharpness Canal brought us to Gloucester docks, the gateway to the river Severn.

Whenever we could escape the routine of daily life we would take off with a group of friends to explore the canals and rivers. Our routes were plotted by the menfolk, invariably finishing up in a pub.

Things didn't always go according to plan. You never knew what hazards might be encountered – such as a steel mattress concealed in the weeds that wrapped itself around the propeller and brought you to a grinding halt. Abandoned shopping trolleys posed another danger. In the winter, stretches of the canal might be frozen. Thank goodness we had a solid fuel stove on board so were able to thaw out our extremities!

We lived on the boat for a while when we married and shared our life with water voles, some nearby peacocks and two friendly swans who pecked at the window if we had overslept. Happy days!
Niva Poole, Truro

Quick puzzle

Can you unscramble this 9-letter conundrum to form a word? You'll find the answer below.

NONIGUILT

A: OUTLINING

Time for you

Eat outside

Now the weather is (hopefully!) warmer, take the opportunity to dine alfresco whenever you can. Whether it's breakfast, lunch or dinner, eating outside has been found to improve concentration, memory and attention while boosting Vitamin D too.

What a good idea!

Make light work of hulling strawberries with a straw. A metal reusable one works best, but a plastic straw will work too. Place the straw at the base of the strawberry and push all the way up until the green stalk and leaves pop out.

Box office blockbusters!

The first James Bond movie, Dr No (1962), didn't get off to the best start – when it went £100,000 over its £1m budget, United Artists were keen to pull it as they felt it wouldn't make a profit, while James Bond creator Ian Fleming described the film as "Dreadful." The rest is history...

Recipe of the week

HONEY-GLAZED PEACH, ROCKET & GOAT'S CHEESE SALAD

Serves: 1
Prep: 10 mins
Cook: 5 mins

1 tbsp extra-virgin olive oil
2 large peaches, cut into wedges
1 tbsp Comvita Mānuka Honey MG30+
150g (5oz) rocket or baby spinach
1 avocado diced
¼ red onion sliced
½ cup goats cheese, crumbled
½ cup almonds, roasted
2 tbsp sunflower seeds
Lime wedges, to garnish
Honey Vinaigrette:
1 tsp extra-virgin olive oil
2 tbsp balsamic vinegar
Pinch of salt
1 or 2 tbsp Comvita Mānuka Honey MG30+

1 Make the honey-glazed peaches: Add oil in a large griddle frying pan and heat on medium-high heat.
2 Once the oil is heated, add the Mānuka honey and peach slices and grill until golden on one side. Remove and leave to cool.
3 In a large bowl, add all the salad ingredients and toss to combine. Top with peach slices and lime wedges.
4 To make the honey vinaigrette, whisk all the ingredients in a small bowl until well combined and drizzle over the salad. Serve immediately.

COMVITA MANUKA HONEY AND LISA HOLMEN

16 SUNDAY

17 MONDAY

18 TUESDAY

19 WEDNESDAY

20 THURSDAY

21 FRIDAY

22 SATURDAY

Precious memories

DEPARTURE TO DENMARK

Everyone thought I was mad when, aged twenty-two, I gave up a great job with Cunard Crusader Travel to go to Denmark to learn the language. I chose Aarhus as it was a university town, it was on the coast and there were not too many English people around to distract me from learning Danish.

I found a cheap room in the centre of town with a shared kitchen and bathroom. A few weeks later I took a job as a cleaner in a hotel as there were no secretarial jobs available and went to language classes three evenings a week.

I stayed for six happy months, travelling around Denmark as well as visiting Germany and Sweden. However, by Christmas I was homesick and realised it would be a long time before my language skills would be good enough to get a better job, so I bought a one-way ticket back to England.

I was sad to leave my new friends behind, but I had made enough money to put a deposit down on a bedsit in West Kensington. While working at the Brompton Hospital as secretary to the matron, I met my future husband at an Anglo-Danish student club.
Fran Pulford, North Harrow

Quick puzzle

Can you unscramble this 9-letter conundrum to form a word? You'll find the answer below.

HAPICAROL

A: PAROCHIAL

Time for you

Stock up on house plants

Having house plants around your home helps to promote wellbeing as well as lower stress and the pop of green really brightens things up. If you're wondering where to start, take a look at succulents, aloe vera and spider plants.

What a good idea!

Brilliant for making stainless steel and brass shine, olive oil is great for bringing your old pots and pans back to life. It's particularly good for polishing stainless steel sinks and taps too and can help prevent water marks forming. Plus, being chemical-free it won't corrode or dull the steel.

Box office blockbusters!

Sunset Boulevard (1950) created a buzz in Hollywood at the time of filming but its script has endured, with the movie's lines regularly voted as some of the best in film. "All right, Mr. DeMille, I'm ready for my close-up" and "We didn't need dialogue. We had faces", are two of these.

Recipe of the week

KOREAN BARBECUE CHICKEN

Serves: 2
Prep: 10 mins
Cook: 30 mins

Vegetable oil
1 clove garlic, chopped
2 tbsp Sun Hee Gochujang
1 tsp chilli flakes
2 tbsp Sun Hee Korean Barbecue sauce
2 tbsp honey
Salt and pepper
300g (11oz) chicken of your choice (wings, breast, or thighs)
220ml (8oz) buttermilk
Handful of chopped chives
200g (7oz) plain flour
Sesame seeds to sprinkle

1 To make the sauce, heat 1 tbsp oil in a medium hot pan and add the garlic. Then add gochujang, chilli flakes, barbecue sauce and mix it together well.
2 Next add the honey, give it a quick stir and add salt and pepper to taste. Season the chicken with salt and pepper before soaking it in the buttermilk for five mins. Add the flour to a separate bowl.
3 Once the chicken has soaked, remove it from the buttermilk and coat each piece in the flour. Heat some more oil in a frying pan and shallow fry the chicken until it's cooked through. Once cooked, toss it in the sauce and serve with a garnish of chopped chives and sesame seeds.
SUN HEE

23 SUNDAY

24 MONDAY

25 TUESDAY

26 WEDNESDAY

27 THURSDAY

28 FRIDAY

29 SATURDAY

Precious memories

HAPPY BLACKPOOL DAYS

This is one of my favourite photos of me and my dad taken on the beach at Blackpool in 1980 when I was fifteen. It was the first year that we had a Polaroid Instamatic camera so we got a good picture instead of the ones in years gone by when heads were quite often chopped off!

We went to Blackpool every July for a week's holiday. My highlight was going to the Pleasure Beach at the end of the week where Dad and I would enjoy trying out each new ride. The log flume was the best and I knew to duck down at the front to avoid getting drenched! I thought it was great to be tall enough to try the Revolution roller coaster with its 360 degree loop.

Another great place we went to was Stanley Park, near the zoo. I liked to jump on the trampolines and have a game of putting or table tennis. On most evenings we went for a stroll on the Central or South Pier and somehow I was convinced I might fall through the wooden slats into the sea below.

These holiday memories are so special because my lovely dad died when I was only eighteen.
Melanie Lodge, Mirfield

Quick puzzle

Can you unscramble this 9-letter conundrum to form a word? You'll find the answer below.

MANNIGOUT

A: AMOUNTING

Time for you

Ditch your electronics at night

For a better night's sleep, stop using all electronics at least thirty minutes to an hour before bedtime. These devices emit an artificial blue light, which makes it more difficult for you to fall asleep. Keep all electronic devices as far away from you as possible when starting your bedtime routine.

What a good idea!

Make a garden self-watering system with an empty glass bottle. Choose one with either a cork or screw top lid and drill a hole in the top. Fill with water, secure the lid and stand the bottle up upside down by inserting the nose into the soil several inches.

Box office blockbusters!

At 5ft 7in, Tom Cruise was three inches shorter than Top Gun (1986) co-star Kelly McGillis – to even them up Cruise wore cowboy boots with lifts to give him more height while McGillis was barefoot for their scenes together.

Recipe of the week

LEMON & MASCARPONE DRAMBUIE TARTLETS

Serves: 6
Prep: 30 mins
Cook: 25-30 mins

175g (6oz) plain flour	50g (2oz) clear heather
100g (4oz) cold butter, cubed	honey
	2 lemons, juice and zest
75g (3oz) icing sugar	2 eggs, plus 2 egg yolks
1 egg yolk	2 tbsp Drambuie
3 tsp fresh thyme leaves, finely chopped	150g (5oz) mascarpone
	4 tbsp heather honey,
250g (9oz) mascarpone	or to taste
50g (2oz) golden caster sugar	**To serve:**
	edible flowers

1 To make the tartlet cases, place the flour, butter and icing sugar into the bowl of a food processor. Pulse until it resembles breadcrumbs. Alternatively use your fingertips to rub together. Add the egg yolk, thyme leaves, and 1 tbsp cold water. Pulse again until it starts to form clumps, or use a butter knife to mix it together, then tip out onto a surface and bring it together with your hands. Wrap in clingfilm and chill in the fridge for 15 mins. Grease 6 x 10cm fluted tart tins.

2 Roll out the pastry to 3mm thick. Using a 12cm cutter, stamp out six rounds from the pastry and place into the tartlet tins, gently push the pastry into the fluted sides. Cut off any excess. Place in the fridge to chill while you preheat the oven to 200°C/180°C Fan/Gas Mark 6.

3 Prick the bases of the pastry with a fork, line with a circle of greaseproof paper and baking beans, and bake blind for 10 mins. Remove from the oven and cool. Reduce the oven to 170°C/150°C Fan/Gas Mark 3.

4 Once the tart cases are cool, beat together 100g (4oz) mascarpone, caster sugar, honey, lemon juice and zest until smooth. Beat in the eggs and egg yolks until combined and smooth, followed by the Drambuie. Pour into the tartlet cases and bake in the oven for 15-20 mins, or until set. Leave to cool. To serve, whip 150g (5oz) mascarpone with the honey and serve on the side. Decorate with pretty, edible flowers. DRAMBUIE

30 SUNDAY

31 MONDAY

1 TUESDAY

2 WEDNESDAY

3 THURSDAY

4 FRIDAY

5 SATURDAY

Precious memories

DARING DIANE

This is me with my cousin Diane at the time of the Coronation in 1953 – I'm the one on the right with my crown almost falling off. Diane had far more poise than me!

We spent a lot of our childhood together. At family parties we were called upon to perform a song or a dance. Diane was taller and slimmer than me and went to dance classes so she was more confident whereas I was quite shy.

Diane was also the daring one of the two of us. At the seaside she once ventured out onto the shoreline where she became stuck in the mud and had to leave her shoes behind to free herself. She was often in trouble with her parents who ran a pub. When they were busy she would pick cigarette ends from the ashtrays and try smoking them.

As her dad was rather strict, Diane preferred coming to my home in the school holidays because my parents were more easy-going. Mum let us make tents in the garden and take over the house with our games.

We were bridesmaids at each other's wedding. These days we keep in touch by WhatsApp and FaceTime and send each other loads of photos of our grandchildren.
Valerie Reilly, Reading

Quick puzzle

Can you unscramble this 9-letter conundrum to form a word? You'll find the answer below.

PANCHOREE

A: CHAPERONE

Time for you

Write a letter to your younger self

What do you know now that would amaze your younger self? Sit down and write it all down in a letter. This exercise offers a period of reflection of your life so far, a trip down memory lane that can even help bring closure.

What a good idea!

Make your toilet sparkle with fizzy pop! Most drinks like cola contain citric and phosphoric acids, which break down stains and get rid of hard water rings. Simply pour the cola round the rim of your loo. Leave overnight and flush in the morning for sparkling results.

Box office blockbusters!

Marilyn Monroe was upset she wasn't invited to director Billy Wilder's wrap dinner for cast and crew of Some Like It Hot (1959). Wilder was mad that the star's erratic behaviour led the film to bust its budget (she took 47 takes to get "It's me, Sugar" correct).

Recipe of the week

PIZZA SCROLLS

Serves: 12
Prep: 45 mins
Cook: 25 mins

1 packet (7g) fast-action yeast
220ml (8 fl oz) warm water
400g (14oz) strong bread flour + a little extra for flouring your surfaces
1 tbsp sugar
1 tsp salt
Jar of tomato pizza sauce
Grated mozzarella cheese
Fresh basil leaves

1 Preheat the oven to 200°C/180°C Fan/Gas Mark 6.
2 Add the yeast to the warm water in the measuring jug. Set to one side while you combine the bread flour, sugar and salt in the large mixing bowl.
3 Add the yeast/water to the dry ingredients and bring together with your hands to form a dough. Tip out onto a floured work surface and knead for 5-10 mins before returning to the bowl and leaving in a warm place to prove for at least 30 mins.
4 Once the dough has doubled in size, knock it back by pushing the air out of the dough with your fist and tip it out onto a lightly floured surface. Roll the dough into a large rectangle, keeping the thickness around 5mm.
5 Use the spoon to spread the pizza sauce evenly all over the dough before sprinkling with the cheese and ¾ of the basil, roughly torn. Roll it all up into a long sausage shape and cut into 12 portions.
6 Place the scrolls swirl side up in the baking tin, leaving a bit of space in between each one, and bake for 20-25 mins until golden. Cool then top with the remaining fresh basil leaves and serve.
EASY PEASY BAKING CAMPAIGN

6 SUNDAY

7 MONDAY

8 TUESDAY

9 WEDNESDAY

10 THURSDAY

11 FRIDAY

12 SATURDAY

Precious memories

A NARROW ESCAPE!

When a colleague heard that I had never had a holiday she kindly arranged for me to stay in her mother's caravan in Rhyl on condition we took great care not to damage anything.

I invited my sister Irene and friends Connie, Doreen and Gwen to join me. We had a great time in glorious sunshine, paddling in the sea and having fun and banter with the boys in the next caravan. We walked three miles every evening to the dance hall in the town.

On the Thursday evening, three of us went to the toilet block for a wash and brush up without Doreen who said she was tired and stayed in the caravan. On our way back, we smelled smoke and I was frantic when I saw it was coming through our door! Doreen was outside with a blackened face. She had turned the oil lamp up high then fallen asleep. Inside the van was black with soot!

The next morning we were up early and first at the camp shop to buy cleaning products. Our last day was spent scrubbing and polishing until the caravan was spotless. We must have done a good job as we returned the following year! That's me, second from right in the photo.
Dilys Bartley, Buckley

Quick puzzle

Can you unscramble this 9-letter conundrum to form a word? You'll find the answer below.

RUNTROVSE

A: TURNOVERS

Time for you

Mindful eating

Pay attention to the taste, sight and textures of your food. When drinking a cup of tea or coffee focus on the temperature, how the liquid feels on your tongue, how sweet it tastes or watch the steam that it gives off. This can help promote better digestion.

What a good idea!

Try this method for cleaning a grubby barbecue. Add white vinegar to a spray bottle and spritz over the grill, then leave to soak. Scrunch up some tin foil and use it to scrub them. You can do this when your barbecue is warm, but not hot.

Box office blockbusters!

When censors first saw the shower scene in Psycho (1960), they deemed it too grisly. Janet Leigh was terrified of showering for a long time afterwards, as she realised how vulnerable and defenceless she was. She would take baths for the rest of her life.

Recipe of the week

CHORIZO SALAD WITH CHICKPEAS, WATERCRESS & PEPPERS

Serves: 2
Prep: 10 mins
Cook: 5 mins

Diced chorizo
1 tin chickpeas
85g (3oz) watercress
1 small tin sweetcorn
1 red and 1 yellow pepper, diced
For the dressing:
2 tbsp olive oil
½ tbsp honey
pinch of chilli flakes
1 tsp white wine vinegar

1 Drain the chickpeas and sweetcorn, put them to one side.
2 Over a medium heat, cook off the chorizo until it's crispy.
3 Meanwhile, make your dressing by simply mixing the ingredients.
4 Toss the watercress, peppers, sweetcorn and chickpeas together and plate. Top with the chorizo and pour over the dressing.
WATERCRESS

13 SUNDAY

14 MONDAY

15 TUESDAY

16 WEDNESDAY

17 THURSDAY

18 FRIDAY

19 SATURDAY

Precious memories

A LOT OF 'FIRSTS'

This photo of me, aged seven, was taken on my first holiday away from home. I stayed with my Aunt Ethel at her house in Bristol.

I was brought up in rural Herefordshire and this was my first experience of a big city. It was the first time I had seen an ice-cream van playing a tune as it came up the street. It was also the first time I had a bath in a proper bathroom because we had no electricity or running water at home.

My aunt spoiled me. She took me out and about most days and I had a lot of treats. We went to Weston-super-Mare and one morning she got me up early as we were taking a coach trip to Cowes on the Isle of Wight. I was excited when we boarded the ferry as I thought we were going abroad! We had egg and chips at a café and I bought my dad a gift of a small brass elephant and a glitter dome for my mum. After all the excitement I slept for most of the return journey on the coach.

After ten days my aunt took me home and although I'd had a marvellous time, I was happy to see my mum and dad again.
Jennifer Phillipson, Hereford

Time for you

Set your intention

Bring your morning cuppa out into the garden and take a moment to set an intention for the day. Think, "This is what I want for today. This is what I want to carry with me through it". Making a hot drink will eventually become a cue and a reminder.

What a good idea!

Grapes make a tasty snack and are also a summer staple. Pop some in the freezer, so you can add them to your glass of wine when needed. They'll help chill it quickly, but without watering it down.

Box office blockbusters!

Walt Disney Studios was on the verge of bankruptcy when producing Cinderella (1950) – if it failed at the box office, it would have spelled the end. Everyone involved gave it their all, and it became a huge hit and helped to finance the building of Disneyland.

Recipe of the week

COCONUT CHILLI & LIME KEBABS

Serves: 4
Prep: 20 mins
Cook: 8 mins

8 wooden skewers, soaked in cold water
Coconut chilli lime marinade
100ml (4 fl oz) soy sauce
150ml (5 fl oz) coconut milk
Juice of 2 limes, keep a little aside for serving
59ml (2 fl oz) apple cider vinegar
59ml (2 fl oz) maple syrup
3 cloves garlic, crushed
1 tsp grated fresh ginger
1 red chilli, deseeded and roughly chopped
Salt and freshly ground black pepper, to taste
Skewers:
1 x 380g (13½ oz) box Fry's chicken-style strips, slightly defrosted
1 red pepper, sliced into thick strips
1 red onion, sliced into thick strips

1 Begin with the marinade. Place all the ingredients into the bowl of a food processor and blitz together until combined. Set aside.
2 For the chicken-style strips, thread the strips onto wooden skewers, alternating with slices of red pepper and red onion.
3 Pour over the marinade and leave to marinate for 15-20 mins (or overnight if possible).
4 Heat the barbecue to a medium-high heat and grill for 5-8 mins, turning often.
5 Remove from the heat and immediately sprinkle with the lime juice that was set aside.

FRY FAMILY FOOD CO

20 SUNDAY

21 MONDAY

22 TUESDAY

23 WEDNESDAY

24 THURSDAY

25 FRIDAY

26 SATURDAY

Precious memories

WONDERFUL MRS BEER

Mrs Beer was a wonderful lady who organised overseas visits for Guides and Rangers. The picture shows a group of girls from Middlesex standing outside the window of a bar in France. I am second from the left. We were the youngest on the trip, probably the most adventurous and certainly we were very noisy.

Everything went smoothly, thanks to Mrs Beer who had every possible angle covered. On one occasion the train we were on was very late and we were in danger of missing our connection. Mrs Beer acted very quickly. She asked the guard to ring ahead to the station and ask them to wait for our train to arrive as she had thirty people on board who needed to change trains. This was done and we scrambled across the line with our suitcases and boarded the second train.

We were a happy lot of young ladies who had fun going on sightseeing trips, shopping and walking on the beach. When this photo was taken we had been out on a visit so we are all wearing our uniforms which included Sea Ranger, Land Ranger and Brownie helper. Didn't we look smart?
June Jones, Ashley Heath

Quick puzzle

Can you unscramble this 9-letter conundrum to form a word? You'll find the answer below.

QUITEIXES

A: EXQUISITE

Time for you

Talk kindly to yourself

We are all too quick to scold or ridicule ourselves. When you next find yourself doing so, stop to tweak your language to how you would talk to a friend. For example, "Don't worry, it's just a spilt drink!" How you talk to yourself can play a critical role in your confidence.

What a good idea!

A broken zip pull doesn't have to mean chucking away your favourite coat or dress. Instead try this quick and easy fix. Remove the broken part and simply thread a paper clip through the zip head in its place.

Box office blockbusters!

Regularly ranked in lists of the top American movies, The Apartment (1960) won five Oscars, including three for Billy Wilder for Best Picture, Best Director and Best Screenplay. It was also the last black and white movie to win Best Picture until The Artist (2011).

Recipe of the week

ALL-THE-GREENS RISOTTO

Serves: 2
Prep: 10 mins
Cook: 30 mins

Olive oil
80g (3oz) leek, diced
2 cloves garlic
200g (7oz) risotto rice
1 vegetable stock cube with 500ml (1 pint) boiling water (+ extra water if needed)
1 courgette, coarsely grated
150g (5oz) cavolo nero, finely sliced
Salt and pepper
50g (2oz) grated vegan hard cheese (optional)
50g (2oz) vegan butter (optional)

1 Heat 1 tbsp of the olive oil in a wide pan over a medium heat. Gently cook the leek for around 5 mins, stirring occasionally. In the meantime, make the stock. Add the garlic and risotto rice to the pan and heat through, stirring continuously for 1 min.
2 Add half the stock, stir thoroughly. Set a timer for 15 mins for cooking the rice (or for the recommended pack cooking time minus 2 mins). Cook the courgette separately in the remaining olive oil to remove any excess moisture, then add to the risotto pan when the timer says 10 mins to go.
3 Stir the rice continuously to avoid it sticking to the bottom of the pan. Add the cavolo nero when the timer says 5 mins to go.
4 When the 15 mins are up, season to taste. It should be al dente, not completely soft. If it's ready, turn off the heat, stir in the vegan cheese and the vegan butter, stirring in gently until deliciously creamy. If you're not using these, stir in some high-quality olive oil. Serve immediately, adding a final drizzle of olive oil onto each individual plate.

NUTRITIONIST PIXIE TURNER FOR WWW.DISCOVERGREATVEG.CO.UK

27 SUNDAY

28 MONDAY

29 TUESDAY

30 WEDNESDAY

31 THURSDAY

1 FRIDAY

2 SATURDAY

Precious memories

A TIDAL WAVE

Here I am, aged fifteen, on holiday in Scarborough with my mum, stepdad and Nan who is sitting by the wall. We were just sitting happily making sandcastles and enjoying the sunshine when it turned unexpectedly into a memorable day.

We hadn't noticed the tide coming in until a freak wave took us by surprise, sweeping right up to us. We had to hurriedly gather up all our belongings and rescue Nan by helping her to get back up on to her feet.

We carried everything back up to our rooms at the b&b where we were staying, right on the seafront. My camera was full of sand and water so Mum took it to a local photography shop where the man took it apart and said it would be alright, but he would have to send it on to us in the post after he had put it back together.

Our landlady was lovely and dried everything out for us ready to pack as we were leaving the next day. We bought her a box of chocolates to say thank you.

I was pleased that the film in my camera wasn't badly affected by the sea water so we have a photo to remind us of that day!
Karen Heathcote, via email

Quick puzzle

Can you unscramble this 9-letter conundrum to form a word? You'll find the answer below.

DOGGIRUNN

A: GROUNDING

Time for you

Write a 'done' list

Instead of a to-do list, try writing down everything you've already achieved, even small tasks like putting in a load of washing. This activates the reward centre in your brain and releases neurochemicals and the hormones that give you a feel-good boost and pleasure in your success.

What a good idea!

Make your windows sparkle with this homemade solution. Fill an empty spray bottle ¾ full with white vinegar and add a big squirt of washing up liquid. Screw the lid tight, shake and spray onto your glass. Leave for a few minutes, then wipe away with a microfibre cloth.

Box office blockbusters!

The Greatest Show on Earth (1952) was the highest grossing film of the year, rewarding its stars for their circus stunts. Betty Hutton and Cornel Wilde (who was afraid of heights) had to learn the trapeze, while Gloria Grahame had to let an elephant rest its foot near her face!

Recipe of the week

DAIRY-FREE CARROT CAKE

Serves: 12
Prep: 20 mins
Cook: 40 mins

For the cake:
150g (5oz) Flora Original
200g (7oz) light soft brown sugar
2 medium eggs
200g (7oz) self-raising flour
2 tsp baking powder
1 tsp mixed spice
175g (6oz) carrots, grated
75g (3oz) pecans, roughly chopped
For the icing:
200g (7oz) dairy-free cream cheese
2-3 tbsp lemon juice
100g (4oz) icing sugar
Pecan halves for decoration

1 Preheat oven to 180°C/160°C Fan/Gas Mark 4. Place the cake ingredients in a large bowl and mix together well until thoroughly combined.
2 Divide between two greased and bottom lined 20cm sandwich tins and bake on middle shelf for 30-35 mins until well risen and a skewer comes out clean. Cool on a wire rack.
3 Prepare the icing by beating together the icing ingredients, except the pecan halves. When the cakes are completely cold, sandwich together with half of the icing and spread the remaining icing over the top of the cake. Decorate with reserved pecan halves.
FLORA

3 SUNDAY

4 MONDAY

5 TUESDAY

6 WEDNESDAY

7 THURSDAY

8 FRIDAY

9 SATURDAY

Precious memories

A SOJOURN IN MALTA

A year after we were married in 1954 my husband was posted from the Wireless Telegraphy Station in Scarborough to Malta on a three-year detachment. We sailed from Liverpool on a troop ship. The journey took three days.

I wasn't too happy in the first flat we found to live in and we moved to a bigger one nearer to where my husband worked. When I became pregnant I missed my family even more and wondered if I'd manage to stay for three years. We could only communicate by post which took quite a while to arrive.

We bought a little car, a Fiat Topalino, to explore the island and found the Maltese people were very friendly and helpful. My daughter was born in May 1956 and my parents came out for the christening. It was the first time my mum had been out of England.

As the pay was much more in Malta we knew that in three years we could save enough money (£2,000) to buy a house which we did when we returned home in 1958, the year my son was born. We'd had our ups and downs, but it couldn't have been too bad as we went back to the island in 1963 and 1966.

Anne Wood, Scarborough

Quick puzzle

Can you unscramble this 9-letter conundrum to form a word? You'll find the answer below.

AISLEGOOP

A: APOLOGISE

Time for you

Dance like nobody's watching

Whatever your ability, anyone can dance and there's a lot to be said for putting on your favourite album and having a boogie on your own. As well as burning calories and other physical benefits, it stimulates endorphins while reducing the stress hormone cortisol.

What a good idea!

This easy peasy way of juicing a lemon means you can squeeze out just the right amount of juice. Use a wooden toothpick or skewer to make a hole in the bottom. Push it in halfway and wiggle, before removing and squeezing! Pop in the fridge to use another day.

Box office blockbusters!

At the premiere of 2001: A Space Odyssey (1968), "whole rows" of MGM executives got up and left as they didn't understand the film. Director Stanley Kubrick meant the film to be "a non-verbal experience", and it became one that younger audiences appreciated (particularly when taking LSD).

Recipe of the week

SAUSAGE & APPLE-STUFFED ROASTED BUTTERNUT SQUASH

Serves: 2
Prep: 20 mins
Cook: 1 hour

Small to medium-sized butternut squash
Olive oil
Salt & pepper
400g (14oz) of pork sausages
2 large apples – chopped into small pieces
1 tsp paprika
1 tsp garlic powder
Parmesan cheese (grated)
Baby leaf spinach
1 small radish, finely sliced
1 cucumber, chopped
1 bag of salad
Fresh thyme
Juice of half a fresh lemon

1 Cut your butternut squash in half, scoop out the seeds and hollow out a little for stuffing. Drizzle with some olive oil and add a pinch of salt and pepper and then throw in the oven at 190°C/170°C Fan/Gas Mark 5 for about 30 mins.
2 For the stuffing, peel the skin off your pork sausages and put into a bowl. Break down the sausage mixture with a fork before adding the finely chopped apple pieces. Season with a pinch of salt, pepper, the paprika, garlic powder and grate in a handful of parmesan cheese, then give it a good mix and leave to one side.
3 Once the butternut squash has been in for 30 mins, take out of the oven and then generously stuff it with the sausage and apple mixture. Grate some parmesan cheese on top and bake in the oven again for another 25-30 mins.
4 Put your salad, baby leaf spinach, finely sliced radish, cucumber in a bowl and drizzle some olive oil and the juice of half a lemon on top. Add a pinch of salt and give it a good mix before plating. Once the butternut squash is done place on top of the salad and then finish off with a sprig of fresh thyme. JAZZ™APPLE

10 SUNDAY

11 MONDAY

12 TUESDAY

13 WEDNESDAY

14 THURSDAY

15 FRIDAY

16 SATURDAY

Precious memories

GREY NOMADS IN OZ

Looking at a map of Australia, my husband and I noticed a road running right round the country and thought it would be a great retirement adventure to check it out.

It took many months, but we were finally granted four-year retiree visas so we sold our house, bid a tearful farewell to family and set off. We had done some research and found a caravan and a towing vehicle which we picked up on arrival in Sydney. After a brief detour to meet up with some of our family from the UK who happened to be visiting Brisbane, we finally set off from Cairns.

We headed inland on long, straight single-track roads, keeping an eye open for road trains which move at high speed and stop for no-one! We passed through fascinating landscapes and saw lots of wildlife. After reaching Darwin we turned south, following the coast road to Perth, from where we went to Adelaide, Melbourne and the Gold Coast.

We loved every minute of being 'grey nomads' and met many other folk who were doing the same thing. We had lots of laughs and remain in touch with some of them. The photo was taken when we stopped at Toowoomba. We lived in Australia for ten years before returning to the UK.
Paddie Dodds, via email

Quick puzzle

Can you unscramble this 9-letter conundrum to form a word? You'll find the answer below.

SEBDIANTA

A: ABSTAINED

Time for you

Be present
Before you get out of bed in the morning, take a moment to do some controlled breathing. Focus on your breath: inhale, exhale, inhale, exhale. Don't force it, just notice it. Focusing on your breath can be a peaceful and enjoyable part of the morning that helps you to be 'present'.

What a good idea!
If you find cleaning paint brushes a chore, try this time-saving trick. In between coats tightly wrap your paint-covered brush in cling film. Alternatively, place in a zip-up sandwich bag, tightly sealing the top. Your brush will stay fresh and ready to use for a couple of days.

Box office blockbusters!

A Star is Born (1954) was Warner Bros' most expensive film but although it was critically acclaimed, it was cut in length to appease movie theatres. It failed to make a profit, leaving Judy Garland, who'd delivered the most emotionally intense performance of her life, broke.

Recipe of the week

CHILLI MIXED BEAN VEGGIE CHILLI

Serves: 2
Prep: 10 mins
Cook: 30 Mins

1 tbsp of rapeseed oil
1 red onion, diced
2 cloves of garlic, crushed
3 carrots, peeled and sliced
1 yellow or red pepper, thinly sliced
1 tbsp of Mr Organic balsamic vinegar
1 can of Mr Organic Chilli Mixed Beans
1 bay leaf
150g (5oz) of basmati rice
Guacamole and fresh coriander, chopped

1 Heat the rapeseed oil over medium heat and saute the red onions until soft. Add in the crushed garlic, then add the sliced carrots and sliced peppers. Cook for a further minute whilst stirring, then deglaze the pan with balsamic vinegar.
2 Pour the Chilli Mixed Beans into the pan, add the bay leaf and give everything a good stir. Simmer for about 10-15 mins on low heat to heat through the beans and soften the carrots and peppers. Add in a little water if needed for consistency.
3 In the meantime, cook the basmati rice according to the pack instructions.
4 When ready, remove the bay leaf and serve the chilli alongside the basmati, fresh coriander and a dollop of guacamole.

MR ORGANIC

17 SUNDAY

18 MONDAY

19 TUESDAY

20 WEDNESDAY

21 THURSDAY

22 FRIDAY

23 SATURDAY

Precious memories

WE LOVED SKEGGY

When my brother and I were little, Butlin's was our family's yearly holiday destination. In those days there were many camps to choose from around the country, but Skegness was our preferred choice.

We arrived by coach and stood in line with all the other happy campers waiting to check in. Our home for the week was a small chalet with bunk beds for us children. We woke in the morning to an announcement that the first sitting for breakfast would be starting shortly. Meals were taken in the large dining rooms, served by our waitress for the holiday. If any of the waitresses was unlucky enough to drop something, the whole room cheered!

Our family spent many happy hours on the sandy beach that was just outside the camp, building sandcastles and paddling in the sea. I remember that we had to go down a flight of steps to reach the beach, but over the years the sand has been washed up and is now level with the top of the wall. Happy days!

Denise Selvey, via email

Quick puzzle

Can you unscramble this 9-letter conundrum to form a word? You'll find the answer below.

PANCHOREE

A: CHAPERONE

September 17 - 23

Time for you

Make your own face mask
If your skin is feeling a bit tired, mix together the juice of one lemon, two tablespoons of sugar and one tablespoon of olive oil for a DIY face mask. This works to exfoliate dead skin cells while hydrating for fresher, healthier-looking skin.

What a good idea!

Forget fancy jewellery cleaners, bicarbonate of soda is great for cleaning tarnished silver. Mix three parts bicarb to one part water until it forms a paste. Using a soft cloth, rub the paste into the silver. Rinse with warm water and then dry and buff until shiny.

Box office blockbusters!

Three years after its release, The Graduate (1967) was the third highest grossing movie of all time, to that date, and Dustin Hoffman became an instant celebrity. Director Mike Nichols felt bad for Hoffman, who was shy: "He seemed exactly like the boy [Ben] in the picture."

Recipe of the week

BEEF & MANGO SALAD WITH PEANUT DRESSING

Serves: 4
Prep: 15 mins
Cook: 2 mins

190g (7oz) SKIPPY® Super Crunch Peanut Butter
4 cloves garlic, crushed
1 tbsp finely grated peeled root ginger
2 tsp lime zest
125ml (4oz) lime juice
455g (16oz) sirloin or rib-eye steak
Baby cos lettuce leaves
75g (3oz) sliced red onion
2 mangoes, peeled, stoned and sliced
490g (17oz) roasted peanuts
60ml (2 fl oz) rapeseed or peanut oil
2 tbsp honey
Salt and freshly ground pepper, to taste

1 To make the marinade, in a large bowl, combine 90g (3oz) peanut butter, the garlic, root ginger, lime zest and 80ml (3 fl oz) lime juice; mix well.
2 Cut the steaks at an angle into 5 or 6 pieces each. Add to the marinade; toss to combine.
3 Heat the barbecue to a medium-high heat. Grill the steak for 1 to 2 mins on each side or until cooked to the desired degree.
4 Arrange the cos lettuce, onion, mangoes and steak on 4 individual serving plates. Sprinkle the salads with the peanuts.
5 To make the dressing, in a small bowl, whisk together the remaining 45g of peanut butter, oil, the remaining lime juice, honey, salt and pepper. Drizzle evenly over the salads.
SKIPPY®

24 SUNDAY

25 MONDAY

26 TUESDAY

27 WEDNESDAY

28 THURSDAY

29 FRIDAY

30 SATURDAY

Precious memories

A SPANISH SOUVENIR

Here is a photo of me on the beach when I was seven years old in 1973. Where has the time gone?

Reminiscing about past holidays, I thought about all the souvenirs we have brought home over the years. When we went to Blackpool we bought our friends sticks of pink rock with Blackpool written all the way through. They were very sticky but minty and lovely.

On trips to the seaside I used to scan the beach for the prettiest seashells to take home with me. If I found one of the conical ones, I'd hold it against my ear, certain that the whooshing sound was the noise made by the waves. I also loved those whirlygig toys that were like mini windmills on a stick that you could push into the sand and watch all the bright colours spinning round.

As a teenager, I went on my first holiday to Spain where there were lots of souvenir shops selling everything from castanets to toy donkeys. My favourite purchase was a Spanish flamenco doll who wore a black and red frilly dress with a headdress of black lace and a veil that flowed down her back. She held a tiny fan and I thought she was absolutely beautiful.
Sharon Haston, via email

Quick puzzle

Can you unscramble this 9-letter conundrum to form a word? You'll find the answer below.

ZAPZAPAIR

A: PAPARAZZI

Time for you

Pick up a childhood favourite

If you don't have it already, find your favourite childhood book and spend an afternoon re-reading it. As well as bringing you a great sense of comfort, it'll transport you back to your younger days.

What a good idea!

Traditional bar soap lasts longer than liquid soap, is better for the environment and has lots of other uses too. Rub a bar over sticking doors and drawers, coat stubborn screws to help them thread easier and rub on door hinges to quieten annoying squeaks!

Box office blockbusters!

Costume designer Edith Head was thrilled to dress Robert Redford and Paul Newman for The Sting (1973), gushing, "Just imagine dressing the two handsomest men in the world." She also recalled how both men wanted to wear blue shirts in the film to emphasise their blue eyes!

Recipe of the week

EASY NO-BAKE BISCOFF CHEESECAKE

Serves: 8-10
Prep: 30 mins (plus chilling time overnight)
Cook: None

170g (6oz) Lotus Biscoff Original biscuits
2 tbsp vegan butter or spread
400g (14oz) plain vegan cream cheese
200g (7oz) Lotus Biscoff Spread Smooth
2 tbsp granulated sugar
2 tbsp Lotus Biscoff Spread Smooth
80g (3oz) Lotus Biscoff Original biscuits

1 Crush the Lotus Biscoff biscuits in a mixing bowl until they are breadcrumb-like consistency. (We did this with a rolling pin or alternatively, you can use a food processor.)
2 Melt the dairy-free spread and combine well with the biscuit crumbs. Transfer the mixture into a loose-bottomed cake tin. Push the mixture down with the back of a spoon to make an even/solid layer.
3 For the filling, mix the cream cheese, 200g (7oz) Biscoff spread and sugar together in a large mixing bowl (this can be done by hand but is much easier using a hand blender). Spoon the mixture on top of the biscuit base and use the back of a spoon to smooth the top. Chill in the fridge overnight.
4 To decorate, melt 2 tbsp Biscoff spread in the microwave for 20 secs or until it is runny.
5 With a spoon decorate the top by creating fine lines of the melted spread (or however else you wish!).
6 Break the remaining biscuits in half and push gently into the cheesecake around the outside.

MARYANNE HALL FROM VIVA!'S VEGAN RECIPE CLUB, VEGANRECIPECLUB.ORG.UK

1 SUNDAY

2 MONDAY

3 TUESDAY

4 WEDNESDAY

5 THURSDAY

6 FRIDAY

7 SATURDAY

Precious memories

OUCH – THAT HURT!

This is such a sweet, innocent picture of me in school uniform sitting on my cherished swing, it is hard to believe how dangerous it proved to be.

The seat was suspended from two metal rods with large hooks at each end so that it could be removed and stored indoors in bad weather. I often took the seat off and pretended to be a gymnast, performing a series of acrobatics on the swing's frame.

I loved to turn upside down and hang there, suspended from the frame. I'm surprised my mother, who usually kept a beady eye on me, didn't discover my antics and scold me, but the swing was at the bottom of the garden.

One day, while engaged in one of my stunts, I caught a delicate part of my anatomy on one of the hooks. I was impaled! My screams brought my mum and my grandma rushing to my rescue. Mum spent hours bathing my 'underneath parts' while Gran tried to calm me down.

Luckily, I recovered quite quickly with no lasting effects, but I had learned my lesson and refrained from daring acrobatics in the future.
Linda Kettle, Portsmouth

Quick puzzle

Can you unscramble this 9-letter conundrum to form a word? You'll find the answer below.

HATINGREM

A: NIGHTMARE

Time for you

Drink herbal tea

It might not be everyone's cup of tea but there are so many herbal flavours available that there's sure to be one you'll like. They have a wealth of benefits that include promoting sleep, reducing stress, keeping skin and hair healthy, lowering blood pressure and soothing a bad stomach.

What a good idea!

Cold black tea is excellent for cleaning grubby windows. Simply pour an extra cuppa with your used tea bag and leave to cool completely. Remove the bag and use this cold tea solution to wipe down your glass. Finish by buffing to a shine with a dry cloth.

Box office blockbusters!

All About Eve (1950) was Bette Davis's comeback film, saying it "resurrected me from the dead." She filmed all her scenes in just 16 days but had to re-record her dialogue from the theatre scene as her voice had been so strained from arguing with her real-life husband.

Recipe of the week

MAPLE BAKED PEARS WITH GRANOLA CRUMB

Serves: 4
Prep: 15 mins
Cook: 25 mins

4 large pears, ripe but a little firm
100ml (4 fl oz) maple syrup
50g (2oz) unsalted butter, diced
4 cardamom pods
1 cinnamon stick
3 strips orange zest
50g (2oz) Lizi's High Protein Granola

1 Preheat the oven to 190°C/170°C Fan/Gas Mark 5. Peel the pears, cut in half and then scoop out the cores. Pour in the maple syrup into a deep baking tray. Place the pears, cut side down, into the tray.
2 Add the diced butter to the tray and scatter over the cardamom pods, the cinnamon stick and orange zest.
3 Bake the pears in the oven for about 25 mins or until tender, turning the pears halfway through cooking. To test the pears are cooked, pierce with a knife, they should present almost no resistance. By the time the pears are cooked the maple syrup and butter should have formed a syrupy sauce.
4 To serve, place two pear halves into a bowl, scatter over a couple tbsp of the Lizi's High Protein Granola and a generous drizzle of the sauce. Serve with a dollop of crème fraiche or sour cream.

LIZI'S GRANOLA

8 SUNDAY

9 MONDAY

10 TUESDAY

11 WEDNESDAY

12 THURSDAY

13 FRIDAY

14 SATURDAY

Precious memories

HAVE JOB, WILL TRAVEL

In the Eighties I had the job of organising incentive trips for a marketing company. We used to take the top sales teams from different companies on fabulous holidays. My job was to fly out to the chosen destinations to find the best hotels and restaurants in advance, then a few months later I would accompany them on their holiday to ensure everything went smoothly.

One mission was to inspect a luxury yacht as a possible venue. It was moored off Antibes and we had full use of it for three days. As we sailed down the French coast I felt like Jackie Onassis! Another time, I was lucky enough to accompany a group travelling on the Orient Express from London to Venice.

Although it sounds like the ideal job, it could be stressful. Realising at Rome airport that the luggage for the whole group had gone astray meant having to rush out and buy 30 toothbrushes and 30 sets of nightwear. One couple summoned me in the early hours because they had fallen out and refused to stay in the same room with each other. I also had to be sure to have a stock of painkillers for people who were suffering from hangovers!
Ann Rowe, via email

Quick puzzle

Can you unscramble this 9-letter conundrum to form a word? You'll find the answer below.

SNACKQUID

A: QUICKSAND

Time for you

Take a digital detox

Take the time to care for yourself without being distracted by endless notifications or falling into the habit of mindlessly scrolling your social media feeds. Why not detox your social media by unfollowing any accounts or people who bring negativity to your feed. Make your digital realm a happy space where you can feel inspired by positive people.

What a good idea!

Disguise scratches in wooden floors and furniture with walnuts. Effective on mild to moderate scratches, rub the nut (minus the shell) across the scratch. Make sure you rub in all directions, so the area is coated in walnut oil. Leave for a few minutes then buff with a cloth.

Box office blockbusters!

Patrick Swayze sure suffered in the making of Dirty Dancing (1987) – not only did he wear a girdle to look thinner, he insisted on doing his own stunts. During the log scene, he injured his knee by repeatedly falling off it.

Recipe of the week

FIG, WALNUT & HALLOUMI SALAD

Serves: 1
Prep: 5 mins
Cook: 5 mins

190g (7oz) of butter lettuce
A handful of walnuts
5 figs, sliced
1 packet halloumi, sliced
80ml (3 fl oz) Comvita UMF 5+ Mānuka Honey
Generous pinch of sea salt flakes
60ml (2 fl oz) extra virgin olive oil
Black pepper to taste

1 Arrange lettuce, walnuts and figs on a serving plate.
2 Heat a non-stick frying pan on medium, add oil, Mānuka honey and halloumi. Sprinkle with salt.
3 Fry until golden on each side.
4 Place halloumi on top of salad with any oil/honey left in the pan as the dressing and serve.
COMVITA MĀNUKA HONEY AND NUTRITIONIST MELANIE LIONELLO

15 SUNDAY

16 MONDAY

17 TUESDAY

18 WEDNESDAY

19 THURSDAY

20 FRIDAY

21 SATURDAY

Precious memories

BOYS WILL BE BOYS

As an only child, I was unaware of how noisy boys could be until I started going to Saturday morning picture shows. I couldn't believe the shouting, stamping, whistling, hooting and jeering that went on. We girls, of course, were much better behaved – most of the time, anyway!

The show started with a cartoon such as Bugs Bunny or Donald Duck followed by a cowboy film with Roy Rogers and his horse Trigger or Gene Autry with Champion the Wonder Horse. Sometimes there was a comedy or a Batman film. But if there was a romantic scene in a film that involved (Heaven forbid!) kissing, there was bedlam as the boys hissed and booed.

Sometimes, halfway through a feature, there might be a sudden whirring noise before the screen went black. This meant that the film had broken which resulted in more pandemonium until the projectionist had spliced it together again and we could continue.

These shows were put on by Associated British Cinemas for children aged between five and sixteen. We had an ABC Minors club badge and our own song to sing at the start of proceedings. Saturday mornings were a highlight of my week and fondly remembered.
Valerie Crossley, Pevensey Bay

Time for you

Ground yourself

Try this grounding technique to re-orientate yourself to the here-and-now and feel calmer about the situation. Breathe in for four seconds, hold for four seconds, breathe out for four seconds, hold for four seconds and repeat. Sometimes overwhelming emotions, worry or anxiety can have you feeling lost and panicked.

What a good idea!

Forget fancy kettle descaling kits, vinegar will do the job just as well. Fill your kettle with a solution of half water and half white vinegar. Leave overnight, empty and rinse thoroughly. Fill and boil the kettle a couple of times before enjoying a cuppa and admiring your handy work!

Box office blockbusters!

On the day filming Cat on a Hot Tin Roof (1958) began, Elizabeth Taylor's husband, Mike Todd, died in a plane crash. After pressure from the studio, she returned to work three weeks later and impressed everyone with her professionalism.

Recipe of the week

LENTIL DAHL

Serves: 4
Prep: 15 mins
Cook: 40 mins

2 tbsp coconut or vegetable oil
1 onion, finely chopped
1 inch piece of ginger, grated
2 garlic cloves, grated
1 red chilli, finely chopped
1 tsp turmeric
1 tsp ground cumin
1 tsp ground coriander
¾ tsp cinnamon
350g (12oz) split red lentils
4 large tomatoes, chopped or 1x 400g tin of tomatoes
400ml (14 fl oz) coconut milk
1 medium cauliflower, cut into florets
2 tbsp Bioglan Superfoods Super Protein
1 tsp salt
1 lime
To serve (optional):
1 bunch of fresh coriander
4 tbsp of coconut yogurt
4 naan breads

1 Add the oil and onions to a large pan and gently fry for 5-10 mins until the onions are soft and beginning to turn brown. Add in the ginger, garlic and chilli and cook for another 2 mins.
2 Stir in the spices and cook for 1 minute to cook them out slightly, then stir in the lentils, tomatoes, coconut milk and cauliflower. Pour in enough water to cover the cauliflower and lentils and bring to a gentle simmer.
3 Add the juice of half the lime (save the other half for serving), then cover the dahl with a lid and leave to simmer for 20-25 mins. When the cauliflower is soft and the lentils are cooked, remove from the heat, and add the Super Protein and stir well, then season.
4 Serve the dahl with fresh coriander leaves, coconut yogurt, lime wedges and naan bread.

BIOGLAN SUPERFOODS

22 SUNDAY

23 MONDAY

24 TUESDAY

25 WEDNESDAY

26 THURSDAY

27 FRIDAY

28 SATURDAY

Precious memories

A GRAND OLD LADY

This photo was taken two years before I was born and shows three generations of my family standing in front of Ethel, our 1937 Vauxhall 14. My motor-mechanic dad looked after this grand old lady with great care.

Ethel had a memorable number plate, ELH 128, but she was far from perfect. She rattled and squeaked her way through country lanes and her brown leather upholstery had seen better days. Only one of her headlights actually worked. There was a little orange indicator on the driver's side but if Ethel turned left the front seat passenger had to lower the window and indicate with their arm.

The speedometer fascinated me as it whizzed round uncontrollably from zero to ninety miles an hour. When I asked, 'How fast are we going?', the answer was always 'About thirty miles an hour'.

It was a sad day when Ethel failed her MOT and a shock to Mum who thought she'd live forever. Ethel's last journey was to the scrap yard where Dad was given some small change for her. The money was shared out and I received sixpence.

Dad soon had his eye on a secondhand Rover 60 for which he paid £155. He christened her Eva.

Hilary Martin, Huddersfield

Quick puzzle

Can you unscramble this 9-letter conundrum to form a word? You'll find the answer below.

INVERQUAG

A: QUAVERING

Time for you

Move your body

Exercising is a quick way to release any pent-up stress you may be holding onto. It doesn't have to be much – a Zumba class, a walk or even an online yoga session can all increase endorphins while improving your mood.

What a good idea!

The small attachment on your vacuum cleaner can be used to clean most lamp shades, but avoid vacuuming if your shade is delicate, or has loose trimmings. Instead, a sticky lint roller is perfect for cleaning the inside and outside of your lampshade in a flash.

Box office blockbusters!

For her role in Bonnie and Clyde (1967), Faye Dunaway had wanted a more casual look so she could perform the action parts with ease, but the costume designer chose glamorous long skirts, beret and a short jacket. It became a fashion sensation and thousands of berets were sold.

Recipe of the week

SMOKY PAPRIKA QUESADILLAS

Serves: 1
Prep: 30 mins
Cook: 5 mins

75g (3oz) Primula Cheese 'n' Paprika
2 tortillas
1 cup red cabbage, shredded
1 cooked chicken breast, sliced
3 tbsp tinned black beans
3 tbsp sweetcorn
1 tsp olive oil

1 Place a generous layer of Primula Cheese 'n' Paprika on a tortilla.
2 Top with cabbage, chicken, black beans, sweetcorn and a final squeeze of extra Primula Cheese 'n' Paprika then put the other tortilla on top to make a sandwich.
3 Heat the oil in a frying pan over a medium heat.
4 Fry the quesadilla on both sides until golden brown. Serve.

PRIMULA CHEESE

29 SUNDAY

30 MONDAY

31 TUESDAY

1 WEDNESDAY

2 THURSDAY

3 FRIDAY

4 SATURDAY

Precious memories

DRESSED IN MY SUNDAY BEST

I started going to Sunday School in the Sixties and loved it. It was held in a big marquee which my sisters and I happened to come across when we were walking in the park. We were invited in and there was a man playing an accordion who taught us children choruses. We listened to Bible stories and if we got an answer right we got a sweet!

We looked forward to going every Sunday. It gave us an opportunity to wear our best clothes including a pair of white lacy gloves that had been handed down to me.

There were lovely outings to places such as Warwick Castle that we might not otherwise have had a chance to see. Growing up in a large family meant there wasn't much money to spare so the Sunday School Christmas party was a real treat.

To record our attendance, we were given a scripture stamp which we enjoyed sticking into a special album. I still own The Golden Bells hymn book awarded to me for good attendance. They were happy days and I learned a lot.

Glenda Edden, via email

Quick puzzle

Can you unscramble this 9-letter conundrum to form a word? You'll find the answer below.

DINGYINIT

A: INDIGNITY

October 29 - November 4

Time for you
Find a penpal
If you used to love receiving letters through the post, why not look for a penpal now? You could stick to people in the same country or even find someone internationally. Visit penpalworld.com to get started.

What a good idea!
Struggling to light your favourite candle as the wick has burnt so low in the jar? Save your fingers and light it with an uncooked spaghetti noodle instead. Dried pasta burns slowly, so you can also use this method to light birthday candles without wax dripping on the cake!

Box office blockbusters!

Filming Poirot's final summation in Murder on the Orient Express (1974) was a challenge – the train carriage wasn't big enough to integrate enough cameras to get all the angles they wanted, so the cast had to sit through the monologue (eight pages worth!) multiple times to get every close-up needed.

Recipe of the week

PRAWN PASTA

Serves: 4
Prep: 5 mins
Cook: 15 mins

300g (11oz) dried linguine
2 tbsp olive oil
300g (11oz) prawns
3 garlic cloves, finely chopped
150g (5oz) Primula Light Cheese
½ lemon, juiced
Handful parsley, chopped

1 Cook the linguine. Heat the oil in a large frying pan over a medium heat. Fry the garlic in the oil briefly until it starts to colour. Add the prawns and fry for a couple of mins. Remove the pan from the heat.
2 In a bowl, mix the Primula Light Cheese, lemon juice and parsley. Stir the mixture through the pasta and garlic prawns. Garnish with parsley and lemon wedges.
PRIMULA CHEESE

5 SUNDAY

6 MONDAY

7 TUESDAY

8 WEDNESDAY

9 THURSDAY

10 FRIDAY

11 SATURDAY

Precious memories

LEST WE FORGET

This is me, aged eighteen, when I joined the Women's Royal Army Corps (WRAC) and was privileged to be one of only two privates who were chosen to attend the 1953 Remembrance Day Service at London's Albert Hall. My parents bought their first television set to watch me in the parade.

Remembrance Day has a special significance for me as my grandfather, Corporal Robert Reed, died at the Battle of the Somme in the First World War. He served in the Northumberland Fusiliers and visiting his grave in France was a very emotional experience.

As a youngster I was in the Air Cadets before going on to join the Territorial Army which I enjoyed so much that I decided to sign up for the regular army.

I'd hoped to be a lorry driver when I joined the WRAC but ended up being a silver service waitress instead. I was posted to Egypt shortly after the Suez crisis, sailing from Southampton to Port Said. I enjoyed my time there, taking part in a range of activities from roller skating to athletics, winning a bronze medal for the high jump. I am still in touch with friends from my time in the army, although it is mostly by phone these days.

Evelyn Norton, Darley Abbey

Time for you

Challenge the 'shoulds'
When you find yourself saying or thinking, 'I should do that', ask yourself, 'Do I really need to?'. Maybe you do or maybe you don't, but so often we do things because it's the way we've always done them, without contemplating whether there's an alternative.

What a good idea!

Make your towels fluffy again with this easy fix. Pop them on a hot wash minus laundry detergent, but with a cup of white vinegar added to the drum or detergent drawer. After, run the cycle again, but this time add a cup of bicarbonate of soda. Line, or tumble dry.

Box office blockbusters!

A Hard Day's Night (1964) may have ridden on the coattails of Beatlemania, but the movie also bolstered it, introducing the group to territories that hadn't yet gone Fab Four crazy. Its box office-busting success led a whole host of Sixties bands to follow suit.

Recipe of the week

CHERRY S'MORES WAFFLES

Serves: 4
Prep: 5 mins
Cook: 5 mins

4 sweet waffles
200g (7oz) milk chocolate, broken into chunks
100g (4oz) mini marshmallows
125g (4oz) Opies Cocktail Cherries, drained and halved
3 tbsp white chocolate chips

1 Place each waffle onto a large piece of tin foil, about 4 times its size. Top with the milk chocolate, marshmallows, cherries and finally the white chocolate chips.
2 Bring the edges of the tin foil up to meet in the middle then scrunch together to make a loose parcel which encloses the waffles.
3 Place on the barbecue or under a hot grill and cook for 4-5 mins until the chocolate and marshmallows have just melted. Enjoy hot straight from the foil.
OPIES

12 SUNDAY

13 MONDAY

14 TUESDAY

15 WEDNESDAY

16 THURSDAY

17 FRIDAY

18 SATURDAY

Precious memories

A PENNY FOR THE GUY

Many of the childhood traditions I remember never happen nowadays, which is not always a bad thing. But does anyone else remember A Penny for the Guy? These days it would be a minefield of child safeguarding issues, but 1961 was a more innocent time.

My friends and I looked forward to it. There was fierce competition to make the best guy to parade around the neighbourhood, hoping to earn a few pennies to spend on sweets and fireworks. People were often extra generous if they thought you'd tried harder.

Planning and collecting material involved raiding wardrobes (usually our dads') for old clothes, a hat and some shoes. The arms and legs were stuffed with newspaper or old stockings our mums saved for us.

That was the year my friend Gillian Wood and I (both aged nine) wheeled our guy out in style in my sister's pram – better than dragging him round the streets between us.

Most guys came to a traditional end, with cheers as they collapsed into the bonfire. That part always made me sad. But not as sad as one friend's dad who loaned us his gardening cap for the parade and found only its charred remains. Oops, we were in real trouble!

Joy Harris, Peterborough

Quick puzzle

Can you unscramble this 9-letter conundrum to form a word? You'll find the answer below.

LATEALIVE

A: ALLEVIATE

Time for you

Release tension

Try a simple tense and release exercise to remove any tension that has been stored up in the day. Work through your body from head to toes and imagine that each body part or organ is tensing and then relaxing. Where you can feel the muscle or body part, physically tense and then let go.

What a good idea!

Most of us have struggled to open a jar at some point in our lives! If all the usual methods aren't working, try this simple trick. Place an elastic band over the lid. Pop on a pair or household rubber gloves and twist. Works every time!

Box office blockbusters!

The visual effects in The Ten Commandments (1956) earned the epic an Oscar and kudos from fellow moviemakers. Steven Spielberg said the parting of the Red Sea scene is the greatest special effect in film history, and he's used the cloud visual effects in his own films.

Recipe of the week

MEXICAN MAC 'N' CHEESE

Serves: 3
Prep: 5 mins
Cook: 15 mins

150g (5oz) dried macaroni
150g (5oz) Primula Cheese 'n' Jalapeños
15g (½oz) red jalapeños in brine, chopped
15g (½oz) tortilla chips, crushed
Handful coriander, chopped

1 Cook the pasta according to pack instructions. Drain and set aside.
2 Mix the Primula Cheese and red jalapeños. Stir the mixture through the pasta, coating it evenly.
3 Top with the crushed tortilla chips and coriander. Serve immediately.

PRIMULA CHEESE

19 SUNDAY

20 MONDAY

21 TUESDAY

22 WEDNESDAY

23 THURSDAY

24 FRIDAY

25 SATURDAY

Precious memories

A HAIRY STORY

I am the girl on the right of this photo. I had dark brown hair and used to dye it black to make me look more sophisticated (or so I thought!).

I worked in the Personnel Office of an engineering firm and one of the apprentice welders told me that he intended to give up welding to become a hairdresser and was going to night school at the local college. I asked him if he could dye hair and he said he would do mine for me if I went to his house.

I duly arrived there one evening after work. He produced a dye which he said was the one used by the trade and proceeded to put it on my hair. Then he put my hair in rollers and sat me under the dryer. He combed my hair out and, to my horror, instead of black it was bright navy blue!

The next morning I went in to work with a headscarf covering my hair. My boss asked why I was sitting in the office wearing a headscarf. When I told him, he burst out laughing and said: "That's what comes of letting a welder dye your hair!"

Jean Maddox, Poynton

Time for you

Practise gratitude

Take some inspiration from Thanksgiving across the pond this week and start a gratitude journal. This is a tool, usually in the form of a notebook, diary or even an app, that provides a space for you to write down the things you are grateful for.

What a good idea!

Banana skins can be used to restore and polish all sorts of leather goods, from handbags and shoes to leather sofas. Rub the inside of the skin over the leather surface, before buffing to a shine with a clean, dry cloth. Be sure to test on an inconspicuous area first.

Box office blockbusters!

Christopher Reeve worked hard to build up muscle for Superman (1978), following a bodybuilding regime devised by Darth Vader actor David Prowse. It was so effective that the shots taken of him at the beginning of the filming had to be retaken to match those at the end.

Recipe of the week

BAKED ALASKA

Serves: 8
Cook: 8 mins
Prep: 1 hour

600ml (1pt) double cream
1 tin condensed milk
125g (4oz) Horlicks Instant
1cm thick slice of Victoria sponge
50g (2oz) raspberry jam
3 free-range egg whites (about 90g (3oz))
180g (6oz) caster sugar (this should be exactly double the weight of the egg whites, so adjust accordingly)

1 Make the ice-cream the day before. You'll only need half the ice-cream for this recipe, so save the rest for another time!
2 Whisk together the cream, condensed milk and Horlicks Instant until soft peaks form. Place into a suitable container and freeze overnight.
3 Take a 500ml pyrex bowl and use the rim as a template to cut a disk of Victoria sponge, then set aside.
4 Line the bowl with cling film so that it overlaps the edges. Firmly press the ice-cream into it to fill the bowl and put back into the freezer.
5 Place the disc of sponge cake onto a parchment-lined oven tray. Top the sponge with a layer of raspberry jam and preheat the oven to 190°C/170°C Fan/Gas Mark 5.
6 In a food processor, whisk the egg whites with 1/4 of the caster sugar until soft peaks form. Turn up to full speed and add the rest of the sugar slowly until thick and glossy.
7 Remove the ice-cream from the freezer and remove from the bowl by pulling the cling film. Place onto the sponge and remove the cling film.
8 Fully cover with the meringue – ensuring there are no gaps where you can see ice-cream.
9 Place in the oven for 8 mins until the meringue is brown at the edges. Serve immediately.
HORLICKS

26 SUNDAY

27 MONDAY

28 TUESDAY

29 WEDNESDAY

30 THURSDAY

1 FRIDAY

2 SATURDAY

Precious memories

NANA'S WELL-KEPT SECRET

This is my mother's great aunt who was always known as Nana. My mum was very close to Nana, but it wasn't until many years after her aunt's death that she told me the family secret.

Nana had confided to Mum that in 1884 when she was twenty one, she had married an army cadet who had been posted to India soon after their daughter was born. He wanted her to go with him, but she refused. He was no ordinary man, being a member of the Fane family who were related to the Earl of Westmorland. He went on to have a distinguished career and was eventually knighted.

Nana was from an ordinary working-class family and I think the prospect of leaving everything familiar behind was too much for her to contemplate.

I have a copy of their marriage certificate but, strangely, the wedding ring that Nana always wore was assayed at a slightly later date. I have found no record of a divorce, but her husband married again in India and had two children.

Nana died in 1949, two years before I was born. How I wish I could have talked to her about the man who nearly changed her life.
Christine Barrow, Plymouth

Quick puzzle

Can you unscramble this 9-letter conundrum to form a word? You'll find the answer below.

NAVELPRET

A: PREVALENT

Time for you

Get cosy

Nothing is as comforting as a warm hug, so make sure to replicate this at home with soft and snug accessories like fluffy socks, a warm jumper or a weighted blanket. The physical comfort will help you feel soothed and relaxed inside and out.

What a good idea!

Added too much **salt** to that stew you're making for dinner? Try adding a raw, peeled potato and cooking for 15 minutes, before removing. Too spicy? Balance the heat with a squirt of honey, or try a tablespoon of plain yogurt or sour cream.

Box office blockbusters!

The famous keyboard scene in the department store is one of the most loved in Big (1988). Both Tom Hanks and Robert Loggia were determined to do the dance themselves after they spotted their doubles on set, ready to takeover. Mission completed!

Recipe of the week

CREAMY APPLE & BUTTERNUT SQUASH SOUP

Serves: 4
Prep: 15 mins
Cook: 15 mins

1 butternut squash, peeled and chopped
1 apple, peeled and chopped
1 potato, peeled and chopped
1 sprig of thyme
1 cup of vegetable stock
1 cup of cream

1 Place the prepared potato, butternut squash, apple and sprig of thyme in a pan and bring it all to a boil
2 Once the vegetables are soft, remove the sprig of thyme and blitz it together. Add a cup of cream and the vegetable stock and cook for a further 3 mins on the hob. Serve with fresh crusty bread.

LIESL MADDOCK FOR JAZZ™ APPLE

3 SUNDAY

4 MONDAY

5 TUESDAY

6 WEDNESDAY

7 THURSDAY

8 FRIDAY

9 SATURDAY

Precious memories

I WAS A SHOWGIRL

Twenty-five years ago my husband, Terry, and I joined a group of volunteer entertainers called Showstoppers, based in Leeds. Terry had worked as a professional entertainer but I was one of the 'talentless totty'. I couldn't sing and I couldn't tap dance, but I looked okay in a leotard, had good legs and could smile to order.

The show was run by a retired dancer and choreographer whose favourite rejoinder if anyone dared to challenge her was: "This is not a democracy!". Every year she planned a variety show with dancing, songs and comedy routines. We'd rehearse for a couple of months before the show ran for four nights at Leeds' Civic Theatre.

After that we took the show on the road, performing at the Grand Hotel in Scarborough, community centres and care homes (where dancers were often required to tap dance on carpet!). One year we had a Noel Coward theme with vocalists singing Mad About the Boy and Don't Put Your Daughter on the Stage, Mrs Worthington. Another time, Terry performed Flash, Bang Wallop, the song Tommy Steele sings in Half a Sixpence.

Two challenges for me were dancing in high heels and having to convert to contact lenses as we weren't allowed to wear specs on stage.
Maggie Goddard, via email

Quick puzzle

Can you unscramble this 9-letter conundrum to form a word? You'll find the answer below.

SLIPAUBLE

A: PLAUSIBLE

Time for you

Set boundaries

Many of us get overwhelmed with gift buying, travel to various family members and not having enough time and space for ourselves. Instead of ending up too tired and burned out to enjoy Christmas, set clear boundaries with people and let them know what you need and what you can and can't do.

What a good idea!

As well as making your nails look pretty, nail polish has lots of uses! Add a little to the end of a thread to keep it stiff when threading a needle. Also, use clear polish to paint over button threads to prevent them fraying and coming loose.

Box office blockbusters!

Although Oliver (1968) cost double its $5m budget, it made $37.4m at the US box office alone. Composer Lionel Bart, who came up with the score, including Consider Yourself and Food, Glorious Food, sold the rights to Max Bygraves for £350, who later sold them for £250k.

Recipe of the week

CHOCOLATE RASPBERRY MOUSSE BOMB

Serves: 6 Prep: 1 hour 30 mins Cook: None

130g (5oz) raspberries	3 tbsp Drambuie
15g (½oz) icing sugar, or to taste	1 tbsp cocoa powder
	150ml (5 fl oz) double
For the shell:	cream
80g (3oz) dark chocolate	To decorate:
For the mousse:	freeze-dried raspberries
2 eggs, separated	You will also need: 3cm
35g (1oz) caster sugar	silicone moulds and 5cm
100g (4oz) dark chocolate	silicone moulds

1 In a bowl use a fork to lightly crush the raspberries, then pass through a sieve to remove the seeds. Sift the icing sugar over the raspberries and mix together. Spoon into the 3cm silicone dome moulds and place in the freezer until frozen solid.
2 Next, prepare the shells. Break the chocolate into pieces and melt in the microwave in 10 second bursts. Allow to cool to room temperature. Brush the melted chocolate into the holes of the 5cm silicone moulds and chill in the fridge to set.
3 To make the mousse, whisk the egg whites in a bowl until foamy. Whisk in half of the sugar and continue to whisk until it forms soft peaks.
4 In a separate bowl, whisk the egg yolks with the remaining sugar. Melt the chocolate in the same way as for the shells then set aside. Beat the Drambuie and cocoa powder into the egg yolk mixture. Pour in the melted chocolate and mix until combined.
5 Whisk the cream until just thickened then fold this into the chocolate and yolk mix, followed by the egg whites.
6 Spoon the mousse into the 5cm moulds, filling halfway up. Take the frozen raspberries out of the moulds and press into the centre of each chocolate mousse. Cover with a little more mousse so they are encased. Place back in the freezer until frozen solid.
7 Remove the mousse from the freezer and release from the moulds about 15 mins before serving, scattering with freeze-dried raspberries.

DRAMBUIE

10 SUNDAY

11 MONDAY

12 TUESDAY

13 WEDNESDAY

14 THURSDAY

15 FRIDAY

16 SATURDAY

Precious memories

A BRAVE NEW HAIRCUT

I was sixteen when I decided a new hairstyle was in order. I took my very long blonde hair to a salon and asked the stylist to give me something new.

Apprehensive about cutting off my locks, she started timidly on a bob, but I told her to cut it short like a boy's and to dye it red. She did as I asked and two hours later I strolled out with no regrets.

On the bus home, I felt a niggling doubt that my dad might be alarmed that his little girl had chopped all her hair off. So I went to our neighbour's house first.

They knocked on the adjoining wall and shouted to my dad that they had a call for him on their phone. When he came they told him the caller had hung up. He said: "Well, what can you do?" before turning to leave. I giggled and he turned back and stared at the person he thought was a stranger, saying: "Michelle?". I could tell from his face that it was one of those 'I'm not angry, just disappointed' moments, which made me feel terrible.

I never did such a thing again in my life!

Michelle Best, via email

Quick puzzle

Can you unscramble this 9-letter conundrum to form a word? You'll find the answer below.

RATTANLEE

A: ALTERNATE

Time for you

Start a new tradition

It's never too late to start a new tradition for the Christmas period that makes you smile every year. This could be setting time aside to make your own cards to send out, taking an annual photo with family in front of the tree or going out for dinner on Christmas Eve.

What a good idea!

If you have a real fire at home, you can save money on expensive firelighters by using tumble dryer lint stuffed into empty cardboard toilet rolls. Dryer lint can also be stored up and used to line outdoor pots in spring, preventing soil escaping out of the drainage holes.

Box office blockbusters!

The cast of Grease (1978) weren't your average high-schoolers – when filming began, Stockard Channing (Rizzo) was 33, Michael Tucci (Sonny) was 31, Olivia Newton-John (Sandy) was 28, while John Travolta (Danny) was 23. Between them, the cast chewed 100,000 pieces of bubble gum during filming – up to 5,000 pieces a day!

Recipe of the week

PICKLED WALNUT CELEBRATION BREAD WREATH

Serves: 8 Prep: 2 hours Cook: 45 mins

500g (1lb) strong white bread flour, plus extra for rolling/kneading
1 tsp salt
350ml (12 fl oz) warm water
1½ tsp fast action yeast
1 tsp caster sugar
3 x Opies Pickled Walnuts, finely chopped
75g (3oz) sundried tomatoes, drained and finely chopped
60g (2oz) parmesan cheese
1 tsp finely chopped fresh rosemary
2 tbsp butter, melted
1 tsp sea salt
1 round camembert, to bake
1 garlic clove, thinly sliced
Fresh rosemary sprigs

1 Sift the flour and salt into a mixing bowl or into the bowl of a stand mixer. Measure out the lukewarm water, stir in the yeast and caster sugar, then leave the yeast to develop for 10 mins until frothy.
2 Pour the yeast water into the flour and mix until a dough is formed. Knead the dough by hand on a lightly floured surface for 10 mins or by using a stand mixer.
3 Cover the bowl with a clean tea towel and leave in a warm place until doubled in size.
4 Knock back the dough then knead in the pickled walnuts, sun dried tomatoes, all but 1 tbsp of the parmesan and finally the chopped rosemary. Divide the dough into 18 even-sized pieces. Roll each piece of dough into a ball.
5 Place a large ramekin or bowl into the centre of a baking sheet. Place the balls of dough around the ramekin leaving a 5mm gap between each ball.
6 Make a second ring of the dough around the first, again leaving a 5mm gap to allow room for the dough to rise. Cover with the tea towel until doubled in size.
7 Pre-heat the oven to 190°C/170°C Fan /Gas Mark 5. Brush the bread rolls all over with melted butter then scatter over the remaining parmesan cheese, sea salt and a little extra rosemary and bake for about 30 mins or until golden.
8 Stud the camembert with garlic and warm in the oven for 10-12 mins until melty. Place the bread wreath onto a board and carefully position the camembert, topped with rosemary, in the middle.

OPIES

17 SUNDAY

18 MONDAY

19 TUESDAY

20 WEDNESDAY

21 THURSDAY

22 FRIDAY

23 SATURDAY

Precious memories

A SUNBEAM IN PANTO

Here I am today, but from the age of seven I was a keen dancer and went to the Maude Dickers School of Dance in Bournemouth. One of the most exciting times in my life came in 1950 when I was twelve and I was one of the troupe of girls chosen to dance in Goldilocks and the Three (live) Bears. Yes, they really were live!

The pantomime took place at a theatre in Southampton and I remember waiting for the train at Bournemouth station wearing my red beret, scarf and gloves. The Sunbeams, as we were called, were away from home for six weeks. We had rehearsals the first week then five weeks of doing the show – two shows a night and two matinées a week. We had to go for a check-up with the school doctor to make sure we were strong enough to stay the course.

We slept in a boarding house, three to a bed and eight of us in each bedroom. (There were a lot of things that wouldn't be allowed today!)

On Christmas Day we had a dress rehearsal, ready to open on Boxing Day. Unfortunately, the electrician was ill so we didn't open until the 27th. **Diane Haigh, via email**

Quick puzzle

Can you unscramble this 9-letter conundrum to form a word? You'll find the answer below.

ROTARYPUG

A: PURGATORY

Time for you

Balance time with yourself and others

While socialising is lovely, it's important to balance your time between yourself and others. If you're feeling overwhelmed, it's okay to say no and take that time for yourself. The rest and rejuvenation will have you at your best when you next catch up with friends or family.

What a good idea!

Did you know tea can help you look more awake? The tannin in tea has anti-inflammatory properties and can help reduce under eye puffiness and dark circles. After making a brew, pop the bags in the fridge. Once chilled place over your eyes and leave for 15 minutes.

Box office blockbusters!

When Bette Davies saw the play of Steel Magnolias in New York, she was determined to be part of the film (1989), envisioning herself as Ouiser, Katharine Hepburn as Clairee and Elizabeth Taylor as Truvy. Instead Shirley MacLaine, Olympia Dukakis and Dolly Parton got the parts.

Recipe of the week

BUTTERNUT SQUASH FILO ROULADE

Serves: 4 Prep: 15 mins Cook: 1 hour 45 mins

Olive oil
1 butternut squash, peeled, de-seeded and cubed
1 tsp paprika
Salt and pepper, to taste
100g (4oz) unsalted cashews
1 onion, finely diced
1 red bell pepper, finely diced
3 cloves garlic, crushed
½ tsp ground nutmeg or allspice
250g (9oz) firm tofu, drained and patted dry
2 tbsp soya sauce
½ tbsp syrup (eg maple, agave)
2 tbsp nutritional yeast
1 tbsp lemon juice
6 sheets of vegan filo pastry
1 tbsp dried or fresh thyme
100g (4oz) baby leaf spinach
Handful mixed seeds (optional)

1 Preheat the oven to 180°C/160C° Fan/Gas Mark 4. Toss the cubed butternut squash in a light coating of olive oil, paprika and salt. Place in a roasting tray in the oven for 40 mins, turning once. Set aside.
2 Roast the cashews in the oven for 5-10 mins. Once browned chop roughly.
3 Reduce the oven temperature to 170°C/150°C Fan/Gas Mark 3-4. Fry the onion in a little oil until soft. Add the red pepper and fry for a further 5 mins.
4 Add the garlic and cook for another minute. Stir through the nutmeg or allspice before crumbling the tofu into the pan. Add the soya sauce, syrup, nutritional yeast and cook for a couple of mins stirring thoroughly.
5 Add the spinach and lemon juice, stirring until the spinach starts to wilt. Stir through the ground cashews, season according to taste. Set aside.
6 Brush each sheet of filo pastry with olive oil and layer one on top of the other in a lined baking tray.
7 Mash the roasted butternut squash then spread onto the filo pastry, leaving space around the edges. Spread the tofu mixture on top of the butternut squash.
8 Fold in both ends of the filo pastry and then roll lengthways, like a Swiss roll. Place the seal face down on the baking tray.
9 Brush with oil and then place in the oven for 40-45 mins or until lightly golden. Remove from the oven, brush with a little more oil, sprinkle seeds over and return to the oven for 5 mins.

VEGAN RECIPE CLUB

24 SUNDAY

25 MONDAY

26 TUESDAY

27 WEDNESDAY

28 THURSDAY

29 FRIDAY

30 SATURDAY

Precious memories

HEAVEN CAN WAIT!

I have fond memories of Sunday School at North End Presbyterian church in Portsmouth. The hall was full of children from four to fifteen years of age. We had hymns and prayers before going to our classes, the girls on one side and boys on the other, while the little ones went to another room. We were all taught the well-known Bible stories before coming together again for a final hymn before going home with our friends.

In later years I became a teacher and had my own group of seven to eight-year-olds. There were some thought-provoking moments such as 'What happened to all the bodies when the floods went down?'.

One little boy started to cry when we attached wings to his tunic to be one of the angels in the Nativity play. Dress rehearsals had gone well so we explained again that he didn't have to say anything, just stand with the others with his arms across his chest.

So what was the trouble? In a very tearful voice, he said, 'I don't want to go to Heaven yet!'. Needless to say, the wings were taken off and he became a tiny shepherd instead.

Happy memories that still bring a smile to my face today.

Doris Whitney, Portsmouth

Quick puzzle

Can you unscramble this 9-letter conundrum to form a word? You'll find the answer below.

MOISTABIU

A: AMBITIOUS

Time for you

Don't strive for 'perfection'

Merry Christmas! There's often a gap between our expectations and reality at Christmas that can cause us a lot of stress and disappointment. Instead of pushing for perfection, remember that perfection is only ever someone's opinion.

What a good idea!

Prevent bobbles on your festive knitwear with this simple trick. Pop your woollens in a bag and place in the freezer for a few hours, before washing following the manufacturer's recommendations. Freezing beforehand keeps the wool fibres stiff and helps prevent bobbles forming in the wash.

Box office blockbusters!

The title track of White Christmas (1954) has sold more than 50 million copies, making it the bestselling single ever! It's almost one of the most covered songs. In the film, Bing Crosby sings it, but not for the first time – he also sang it in 1946 film Blue Skies.

Recipe of the week

CHOCOLATE ORANGE TEAR & SHARE WREATH

Serves: 10
Prep: 5 mins
Cook: 40 mins (plus proving time of 2 hours)

600g (1lb 3oz) strong flour	(to grease tin)
50g (2oz) caster sugar	1 tbsp cocoa powder
1 tsp salt	2 tbsp caster sugar
1 packet (7g) dried yeast	100g (4oz) dark chocolate,
2 large oranges (for zesting)	finely chopped
100g (4oz) unsalted butter	100g (4oz) dark chocolate,
200ml (7 fl oz) milk	melted
2 eggs	Orange zest
Unsalted butter, softened	24-27cm bundt tin

1 In a large mixing bowl, combine the flour, 50g (2oz) caster sugar, salt, dried yeast and zest of 2 oranges. Gently heat the butter and milk together in a pan just until the butter has melted. Allow to cool slightly, then beat in the eggs.

2 Pour the liquid mixture into the dry ingredients and bring together to form a sticky dough. Tip out onto a floured worktop and knead for at least 10 mins until smooth and springy to touch. Return the dough to the mixing bowl, cover and leave in a warm place for an hour or until doubled in size.

3 Grease a bundt tin with butter and set it to one side. In a small bowl, mix together the cocoa powder and 2 tbsp caster sugar, then tip the mixture into the greased tin and move around the edges to coat. Divide the dough into 30 pieces at 40g each and roll into balls.

4 Arrange a layer of dough balls in the base of the tin, evenly sprinkle half of the chopped chocolate on top, then place the remaining dough balls on top to create a second layer, sprinkling with the remaining chopped chocolate. Cover the bundt tin and leave in a warm place to prove for an hour.

5 Heat the oven to 180°C/160°C Fan/Gas Mark 4 and bake the wreath for 30-35 mins until risen and golden. Allow to cool until just warm. Turn the wreath out onto a serving plate, drizzle with melted chocolate and decorate with orange zest.

CARR'S FLOUR

31 SUNDAY

1 MONDAY

2 TUESDAY

3 WEDNESDAY

4 THURSDAY

5 FRIDAY

6 SATURDAY

Precious memories

LIFE IN A PREFAB

When I was two we moved into one of the prefabs that were erected as temporary housing after the war. Our little dwelling was very basic. There was no central heating, just a very small stove in the living room. Once it was lit, lumps of coke were added and the doors were opened slightly to let out the heat. It was very cosy in winter with the curtains drawn.

All the fitted furniture such as wardrobes, airing cupboard and larder were made of metal and painted. The window frames were also metal and in the winter they used to ice up on the inside in pretty patterns.

At Christmas when the plum pudding was being made I was allowed, as a treat, to add a sixpenny piece to the mixture before scraping out the empty bowl. Whoever found the sixpence in their pudding on Christmas Day had to make a wish.

As simple as it was with no car, television or phone, we had a comfortable lifestyle. In time, the neighbourhood became a small community. Neighbours chatted over the garden fence and everyone helped everybody else as best they could.

I have very happy memories of the fifteen years we lived there before the prefabs were finally demolished.
Angela Morris, Ringwood

Quick puzzle

Can you unscramble this 9-letter conundrum to form a word? You'll find the answer below.

QUIETRISE

A: REQUISITE

Time for you

Create a mood board

Whether you want to use Pinterest or do things the old fashioned way with a piece of paper, now is the perfect time to create a mood board, ready for the year ahead. Also known as a vision board, this can also help bring you clarity over what you want for yourself.

What a good idea!

Reuse your household recycling to safely store away your Christmas decorations. Egg boxes are great for housing small baubles, while cardboard bottle holders from the supermarket are great for storing bigger tree ornaments. To keep them tangle free, wrap tree lights around old bits of cardboard.

Box office blockbusters!

The cast and crew of Dr Zhivago (1965) suffered for their art – the cast wore replica underwear even though it was never seen on screen, and their thick coats and winter hats were stifling in the 30-degree heat of Madrid. The snow was created by crushing marble into powder.

Recipe of the week

MUSHROOM TARTLETS WITH CARAMELISED ONION MARMALADE

Serves: 12
Prep: 10 mins
Cook: 25 mins

1 tbsp butter
250g (9oz) chestnut mushrooms, cleaned and thinly sliced
1 tbsp crème fraîche
3-4 tbsp fresh thyme leaves, finely chopped
12 slices of thin sliced white sandwich bread
Butter, for spreading
4 tbsp Tracklements Caramelised Onion Marmalade
100g (4oz) grated gruyère or cheddar

1 Preheat the oven to 220°C/200°C Fan/Gas Mark 7. In a frying pan, heat the tbsp of butter, add the mushrooms and stir until the moisture has evaporated and the mushrooms are golden. Turn off the heat, stir in the crème fraiche.
2 Add all but a sprinkling of thyme and chill the mixture in the fridge.
3 Cut 8cm circles out of the bread with a biscuit cutter (or a glass or a jam jar). Spread butter on one side of the circle and put it, butter side down, in a tartlet tin so that the bread creates a base and sides for the tartlet.
4 Add a small teaspoon of Caramelised Onion Marmalade to each tartlet, top with the mushroom mixture and a sprinkling of grated cheese.
5 Bake for 10-15 mins until golden and bubbling. Sprinkle over the rest of the thyme and serve hot or cold.
TRACKLEMENTS

2023 year-to-view calendar

JANUARY						
M		2	9	16	23	30
Tu		3	10	17	24	31
W		4	11	18	25	
Th		5	12	19	26	
F		6	13	20	27	
Sa		7	14	21	28	
Su	1	8	15	22	29	

FEBRUARY						
M		6	13	20	27	
Tu		7	14	21	28	
W	1	8	15	22		
Th	2	9	16	23		
F	3	10	17	24		
Sa	4	11	18	25		
Su	5	12	19	26		

MARCH						
M		6	13	20	27	
Tu		7	14	21	28	
W	1	8	15	22	29	
Th	2	9	16	23	30	
F	3	10	17	24	31	
Sa	4	11	18	25		
Su	5	12	19	26		

APRIL					
M		3	10	17	24
Tu		4	11	18	25
W		5	12	19	26
Th		6	13	20	27
F		7	14	21	28
Sa	1	8	15	22	29
Su	2	9	16	23	30

MAY						
M	1	8	15	22	29	
Tu	2	9	16	23	30	
W	3	10	17	24	31	
Th	4	11	18	25		
F	5	12	19	26		
Sa	6	13	20	27		
Su	7	14	21	28		

JUNE					
M		5	12	19	26
Tu		6	13	20	27
W		7	14	21	28
Th	1	8	15	22	29
F	2	9	16	23	30
Sa	3	10	17	24	
Su	4	11	18	25	

JULY						
M		3	10	17	24	31
Tu		4	11	18	25	
W		5	12	19	26	
Th		6	13	20	27	
F		7	14	21	28	
Sa	1	8	15	22	29	
Su	2	9	16	23	30	

AUGUST					
M		7	14	21	28
Tu	1	8	15	22	29
W	2	9	16	23	30
Th	3	10	17	24	31
F	4	11	18	25	
Sa	5	12	19	26	
Su	6	13	20	27	

SEPTEMBER					
M		4	11	18	25
Tu		5	12	19	26
W		6	13	20	27
Th		7	14	21	28
F	1	8	15	22	29
Sa	2	9	16	23	30
Su	3	10	17	24	

OCTOBER						
M		2	9	16	23	30
Tu		3	10	17	24	31
W		4	11	18	25	
Th		5	12	19	26	
F		6	13	20	27	
Sa		7	14	21	28	
Su	1	8	15	22	29	

NOVEMBER						
M		6	13	20	27	
Tu		7	14	21	28	
W	1	8	15	22	29	
Th	2	9	16	23	30	
F	3	10	17	24		
Sa	4	11	18	25		
Su	5	12	19	26		

DECEMBER						
M		4	11	18	25	
Tu		5	12	19	26	
W		6	13	20	27	
Th		7	14	21	28	
F	1	8	15	22	29	
Sa	2	9	16	23	30	
Su	3	10	17	24	31	

RELAX & UNWIND

A kiss is just a kiss

Writer Marion Clarke and Yours readers recall the time that we realised boys weren't there just to get on our nerves

To be honest I am rather hazy when it comes to remembering my first kiss. It might have happened when we played kiss chase at primary school (were you the one, Ian Snow?) or maybe on my first proper date when I was 12. But all I recall about that evening is that my beau (I think his name was Brian) wore his Scout uniform and we played a round of crazy golf followed by fish and chips wrapped in newspaper. We probably did nothing more daring than holding hands...

I was a late starter compared with **Avril Wallis** who was only eight when she attracted the attention of a schoolmate while returning from playtime in the school yard.

"As I walked into the hall, a boy stepped out from behind one of the doors, grabbed me and planted a kiss on my cheek before releasing me with a big smile on his face. Whether it was the result of a dare I never knew, but it was quite a topic of conversation for the rest of the day."

Mrs E Jones was also still at primary school when she received a note from a boy in her class that said, 'Can we meet by the bike shed tomorrow playtime for a kiss?'

"The next morning my mum found the note in my coat pocket. Mortified, I ran upstairs, locked myself in the bathroom and wouldn't come out. I was teased for ages by all the family, neighbours and school friends."

Angela Patchett's first kiss was accompanied by a proposal of marriage, although she had to turn her suitor down for reasons that made sense at the time. "I was just 12 years old and out playing with a boy called Sidney who was showing off by hanging upside down on some scaffolding. He suddenly jumped down and kissed me full on the lips, saying, 'I love you. When we grow up I shall marry you'.

"'What is your surname?' I enquired. 'Burrows,' he replied. 'Well!' I exclaimed, 'my name is Warren'. He replied, 'That's good. We can make lots of little rabbits together'. I left quickly and ran home for my tea."

There was a happier ending for **Doreen Smith**. "I was five years' old when I went with Mum and Dad to visit Mum's sister and her son, who was eight.

"He took me to the shed to show me a boat he had made for me to sail in the park. Years later we got married and he reminisced, 'I made you a boat and kissed you and you didn't pull away'. We were married for 29 years and had lots of kisses after that first one!"

Many youngsters learned a lot about kissing techniques by studying close-ups of their favourite film stars – not always a good idea, as **Margaret Rymer** discovered...

"My first kiss happened at the Saturday morning flicks when I was about 12. My boyfriend put his arm around my shoulders and kissed me on the lips. Quick as a flash, I slapped him across his face. He drew back, horrified. I was quite sorry as I had only done it to copy a scene in a film I'd seen which I thought was wonderfully dramatic.

"That poor lad never tried to kiss me again. And needless to say, I never tried that trick again because it looked better than it felt!"

There were other hazards to kissing as **Pamela Standbridge** learned when a pesky cold sore almost ruined her budding romance. "I was 18 and had been going out with a quiet, shy boyfriend for six weeks. We were saying goodnight at my garden gate when he suddenly said, 'I was going to kiss you goodnight tonight, but you have a nasty cold sore'.

"That cold sore on my bottom lip lasted another three weeks, but it all turned out OK. We married and had three wonderful daughters."

For many of us, party games were our first introduction to being kissed and, as **Pat Berkshire** admits, it wasn't a bit romantic. "I was about 13, at a birthday party, and Postman's Knock was the game. I was so embarrassed when I was called, I blushed furiously and presented my cheek to be kissed. I think the boy was quite happy to peck my cheek and escape back to the company of the party."

But it was a party game that rescued **Barbara Nuttall** from the unwanted attentions of the local Romeo: "When I was 15 I had a birthday party at home. We played Spin the Bottle. When the bottle stopped facing you, the spinner had to give you a kiss. This worked out well for me because the boy from our street who had been pushing love letters through my door thankfully went off with the girl he kissed." That's teenagers for you – so fickle!

Some over-enthusiastic boys simply didn't get the hang of kissing at all. Such a one was a lad called Dougie that **Freda Minns** met at a dance. "Every time I went out with him, Mum would say, 'Been out with Dougie again?'. When I asked her how she knew, she said, 'You go out with make-up on but come home with a clean face'. Every time he kissed me, his tongue would wash my face. I didn't like that kind of kissing so I packed him in."

QUICK CROSSWORD 1

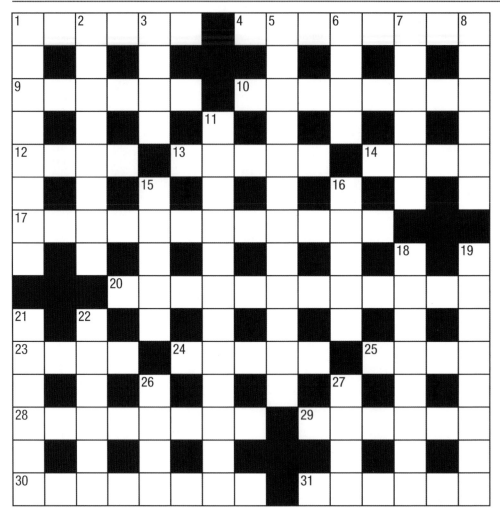

ACROSS
1 Common flatfish (6)
4 Grope (for) (8)
9 Artists' tripods (6)
10 Adieu (2, 6)
12 Jane - - -, Charlotte Brontë novel (4)
13 Charabanc (5)
14 Sear (4)
17 Late creator of Dinnerladies (8, 4)
20 Small European pigeon (8, 4)
23 - - - Woodyatt, longest-serving actor in EastEnders (4)
24 Rustic, countryman (5)
25 Squad selection (4)
28 Finland's capital (8)
29 Body of water within an atoll (6)
30 Herb of remembrance (8)
31 Aphrodite's mortal lover (6)

DOWN
1 Cure food to resist decay (8)
2 Non-figurative art form (8)
3 Young male horse (4)
5 Parish administrator (12)
6 Zenith, acme (4)
7 Decoratively perforated shoe (6)
8 Boy's task? (6)
11 Welfare officer (6, 6)
15 Section of the large intestine (5)
16 Friend of Big-Ears and Mr Plod (5)
18 Decline in status (8)
19 Bus route's end (8)
21 Christian priest's term of address (6)
22 1980s US TV show with Larry Hagman as JR Ewing (6)
26 Having determination, resolute (4)
27 Extol (4)

QUIZ 1

1 What does "www" stand for in a website browser?

2 What geometric shape is generally used for stop signs?

3 Which animal can be seen on the Porsche logo?

4 Which country consumes the most chocolate per capita?

5 What was the first toy to be advertised on television?

6 What are the names of Cinderella's stepsisters?

7 Which country touches the Indian Ocean, the Arabian Sea, and the Bay of Bengal?

8 Who was the first woman pilot to fly solo across the Atlantic?

9 Which is the only edible food that never goes bad?

10 The unicorn is the national animal of which country?

11 Which monarch officially made Valentine's Day a holiday in 1537?

12 The name of which African animal means "river horse"?

13 How long is an Olympic swimming pool (in metres)?

14 What is the rarest M&M colour?

15 What is the most consumed manufactured drink in the world?

Were you right? Turn to page 182 for the answers

Shedding the past

Fond memories make Maggie reluctant to take all her old junk to the dump

Maggie gazed despairingly at the contents of her shed. Old bicycles, a go-cart, a rusty lawnmower, garden tools – the list was endless. The lad who did her garden brought his own tools and her children had outgrown their bikes long ago. The grandchildren had played with the go-cart but now it had a wheel missing and needed a lick of paint.

The barbecue hadn't been used since her husband, Bob, had died. He had loved cooking barbecues for the family and she had loved the hubbub of children racing around, giggling and shouting.

She sighed. Those days were gone. Her family lived too far away to visit often. She was invited to stay for Christmas and Easter, but the grandchildren were young adults now with lives of their own. No, she wouldn't feel sorry for herself! She would have a big clear out and get rid of all the unwanted things that brought back memories.

Maggie went to the charity shops. They shook their heads. "Sorry, love, unless things are in a good condition we can't take them. Try a clearance company."

She was in the village shop one morning, explaining her problem to the owner when a woman behind her said: "Excuse me, I couldn't help overhearing, but have you tried the school? They are always on the lookout for stuff."

"Thank you, I will," said Maggie.

She lived near to the primary school that she had attended herself, as had her own children. Her spirits were always lifted by the happy clamour of the youngsters at playtime. She pushed open the gate and crossed the empty playground.

The secretary greeted her politely. "How can I help you?"

Maggie explained.

The girl looked dubious. "Well, I'll have to ask. Someone will let you know."

Maggie could see that she thought it was an odd request and felt foolish. She wondered if the girl would even bother to pass on the message.

Ten days later she heard a knock on the door. She opened it to see the school's headmistress. "I understand you have some things we might like?" she enquired after introducing herself as Eleanor Jones. "I'm sorry I haven't been round before, but it's been a busy week."

"Do come in," said Maggie.

She took Eleanor through to the garden and showed her the contents of the shed. "I'm sure some of this could still be useful. I don't want it all taken to the dump."

Eleanor said: "Oh, you won't need to do that. The school has a very active PTA and I'm sure some of the dads – and the mums – could work wonders with these things."

Maggie made coffee and they chatted. She told Eleanor of her own long connection with the school.

The following week two fathers from the PTA came with a van and emptied the shed, driving off with a cheerful wave. And that, thought Maggie, was that. All that remained of my family gone. Empty shed, empty heart, she thought ruefully. She made a cup of tea to cheer herself up.

The days passed and she got on with her usual routine. She had a lovely call from her daughter to say they'd booked a cottage for the holidays and wanted Maggie to join them.

"Empty shed, empty heart, she thought ruefully"

Then one afternoon the clatter of the letterbox made her jump. It was too late in the day to be the postman.

What looked like hundreds of letters lay on the mat, all addressed in childish handwriting. She took them through to the sitting-room to open them.

'Dear Mrs Atkins,' the first one read, 'Thank you so much for lovely things you gave the school, luv Emily'. The next one was from Brian (year 2), 'Dear Mrs Atkins, thank you for the things from your shed'.

Some of the letters were decorated with drawings of bicycles and go-carts. 'Dere Mrs Atkins, we have raised a lot of munny from the things you sent,' wrote Olivia and Alison's letter said, 'My dad bought yore bike and mended it for me to ride at weekends'.

Maggie felt close to tears.

There was a note from Eleanor. 'Dear Maggie, your kind donations raised much-needed funds for the school. We sold everything except the barbecue which we hope to use at our summer fête. We'd be delighted if you would be our guest of honour and officially open proceedings at 2pm on July 10th. Best wishes, Eleanor'.

A few weeks later Maggie, wearing her best dress and feeling a bit self-conscious, cut the ribbon to loud cries of 'hooray'. Everyone treated her like royalty and she had a wonderful time.

Eleanor asked if she would come and talk to the children about her time at school. They were compiling a history of the village and wanted to know how things had changed.

On her way home, Maggie almost skipped along. If she ever felt she was missing her own family, she could always get those letters out. Just reading 'mrs atkins, you are so wunnerful, love archie xx' would make her feel better. Just wunnerful, in fact.

A tin bath by the fire

Writer Marion Clarke and **Yours** *readers relive the time when ensuite bathrooms were something we could only dream of...*

We were lucky enough to have a bathroom and running hot water, but bathtime was only once a week – usually on Sunday, ready for school on Monday. The part I dreaded was having my hair washed which meant stinging eyes from the shampoo, rough drying with a towel followed by the agony of having all the tangles combed out. Ouch!

Things were very different for **Barbara Smith** who was one of six children: "On Friday night the tin bath was put in front of the fire in the living room and filled with water from a boiler in the kitchen. We were bathed two at a time with the water being topped up after each session. Mum washed us and Dad dried. After a cup of milk and a slice of bread, Dad gave us a fireman's lift up the stairs to bed."

Edwina Jones's family had a similar routine. "Once my two younger sisters had been bathed, dried and put in warmed vests, liberty bodices and pyjamas, it was my turn. By then the water had gone cool and I wanted to get out quickly. I caught my foot on the edge of the bath, it tipped over and water flooded all over the floor. I had a smacked bottom for that!"

One bar of soap went a long way in **Theresa Ellis's** family: "Eight children went one after the other into the same water with the same flannel in a freezing bathroom and nobody ever caught anything from any of the others. The secret was the big bar of carbolic soap that killed every germ in its wake, then went on to scrub the clothes on Monday and the floors on Friday before finding its way back into the bath on Saturday!"

Having a bath in front of the fire in the kitchen was the highlight of Saturday night for **Brenda Watt**, but there was a downside: "No bathroom also meant having an outside toilet. During the day I hated my trips to the toilet because of the spiders and the daddy-long-legs on the walls. At night I went armed with a torch and my faithful dog Pip who must have dreaded me waking him up to be my escort."

Having a bathroom was not always better than a cosy soak in front of the fire, as **Sylvia Washington** discovered: "Even when we had a proper bath installed in our cottage, there was no heating. In the winter months a paraffin stove was lit, but it was barely adequate. On one occasion it burst into flames and a cloud of thick black smoke filled the room. My dad quickly threw a sack over it and ran outside to put it out in the snow."

In 1962, **Caroline Thompson's** family moved to a farm in Aberdeenshire: "We had no electricity, no bathroom and water was heated by a coal fire and back boiler. Poor Mum! She used to bathe me and my two brothers (all under five) in the scullery sink. It was a big, deep sink for washing clothes and we'd stand on the draining board while she dried us."

After **Janet Russell's** mum had done the laundry, she used the soapy water to wash Janet: "I can remember as a child being put in the 'dolly tub' after Mum had washed the whites. I think she used Acdo washing powder. My skin is OK so it couldn't have done me any harm!"

Sue Payne's happiest bathtime memory was on the eve of her wedding in 1966. "My family had just got a long (person-sized) tin bath. I boiled kettles and saucepans of water, sprinkled in lavender-scented bath cubes, put on a shower cap to protect my newly set hair and indulged in a lovely long bath in the warmth of the kitchen heated by the gas stove. Absolute bliss."

When **Pat Rose** got married in the Sixties, she and her husband rented rooms in an old house: "There was a bath in my tiny kitchen, hidden under a hinged worktop. To have a bath, I had to lift up the worktop and secure it against the wall with two large hooks. It was rather surreal to sit in the bath surrounded by my washing machine, cooker and kitchen cabinet."

Pat Warminger also started married life in a rented flat with no bathroom: "When we got our own home I ran straight up to the lovely new bathroom and climbed fully clothed into the empty bath just to see what it was like!"

For folk with no bathroom, a visit to the public baths was the usual option, as **Sylvia Elliott** recalls: "It cost fourpence and

you were given a towel and a piece of soap. The attendant (who looked like an army sergeant) put the water in from outside the cubicle. You only had a few inches so you had to be quick before it went cold. If you took longer than the time allowed, the attendant would bang on the door!"

On his weekly visit to the public baths, ten-year-old **Alan Dury** liked to sing. Once, in the middle of his rendition of Oh Shenandoah, someone joined in with 'Far away, you rolling river...' "Feeling embarrassed, I stopped. 'Carry on!' called out a voice – so we continued in unison."

Bet that had the attendant banging on the cubicle door!

Best latte in town

Making new friends after moving to the coast is not as easy as Brenda had hoped

Brenda felt she'd made the right decision moving to a seaside village. Retiring to the coast had always been her husband's plan, but after she was widowed she decided go ahead on her own. Her son lived not too far away and she would be kept busy helping her friend Monica in her gift shop.

So far she was enjoying her new home, but she still hadn't met many people. There was a photography club in the village and Brenda was keen to join it. With this in mind, she headed out for a walk along the beach with her camera.

Spotting a café on the promenade, she decided to stop for a coffee. Monica had already pointed out the owner to her, mentioning (not very subtly) that he was single and made the best latte in town.

As she pushed open the door, he glanced up. Tall, with attractively greying hair, he had nice brown eyes, but it seemed his looks weren't matched by his personality. He looked distinctly gloomy.

Brenda attempted to break the ice. "My friend says your coffee is highly recommended so I'm here to put it to the test," she said brightly.

He didn't smile. "Are you trying to say that you wish to buy a coffee?"

"Um, I suppose I am," Brenda mumbled.

"To have in or take away?"

"I'll have a takeaway, please, if that's alright?"

"Of course," he replied stiffly. "But please be sure to dispose of your cup responsibly."

Brenda bridled. "I always do. I'm a very responsible person."

He appeared to sense that he'd gone too far and managed a faint smile: "I'm sorry, but you'd be amazed how much rubbish visitors leave on the beach and I don't like getting the blame for some of it."

As she left the café, Brenda glanced at his faded advertising posters peeling off the wall.

"He really has got on the wrong side of you. Honestly, he's usually very nice"

organises the monthly beach clean but there's a shortage of volunteers," Monica defended him.

"I'm not surprised, with his attitude. And he'd attract more customers if he put up better posters, in my opinion."

Her friend laughed: "He really has got on the wrong side of you. Honestly, he's usually very nice."

"Well, in that case, I'll give him a second chance," Brenda conceded.

She called in at the café a few times after that, but didn't see Andy as he was off duty. After one of these visits, she was struck by an idea which required taking her camera down to the beach again. She was taking a photo, balanced precariously on a slippery rock, when she heard a voice.

I t was Andy, gesturing towards the remains of someone's picnic nearby. He said: "I hope you aren't going to leave that there. I thought a responsible person like you would know better."

He was actually smiling but Brenda, struggling to keep her balance in the blustery wind, took exception to his remark. She snapped: "Of course not! I don't know why you've got it

Further on, she noticed a bank of large recycling bins and smiled to herself. She imagined the café owner badgering the council to put them there.

As she was helping Monica in her shop the next day, Brenda told her about the lecture she'd been given about disposing her coffee cup responsibly. "He was very grumpy!" she laughed.

"Andy?" Monica asked. "I don't think he's grumpy."

"Well, he was yesterday. Moaning about visitors and their rubbish."

"You must have caught him on a bad day because he really needs the visitors. He

in for me."

"I was only joking," Andy said sheepishly. "I think we got off on the wrong foot."

He turned and strode away along the beach, hands thrust deep in his pockets. Brenda felt guilty – he had seemed genuinely apologetic. She called after him: "Well, you certainly haven't gone about things in the right way. Hey, listen, I've thought of a plan you might find interesting."

But he was already out of earshot and the wind blew her words away.

A few days later, Brenda got the perfect opportunity to tell Andy her plan. He was alone behind the counter so she was able to spread out the poster she'd designed.

"There you are," she said. "That is what I was doing when you saw me on the beach."

He studied the poster carefully. Above her photograph of the picnic remains on the beach she had put the heading 'The Other Side of Visitors' and underneath there was an appeal for volunteers to join the monthly beach clean.

"Wow! I didn't know you were working on this," Andy said. "Why didn't you say?"

"You hardly gave me a chance," Brenda told him. "And I don't mean to be rude, but your posters for the café could do with a redesign."

"That's true," Andy grinned ruefully. "And this one is great. We need to get some copies to put up around the village."

"I hope they'll attract lots of volunteers. I'd like to be one of them, if you'll have me?"

Andy looked surprised. "Really? Even though I've been so moody?"

"Absolutely," Brenda laughed. "I'm sure there is another side to you as well!"

QUICK CROSSWORD 2

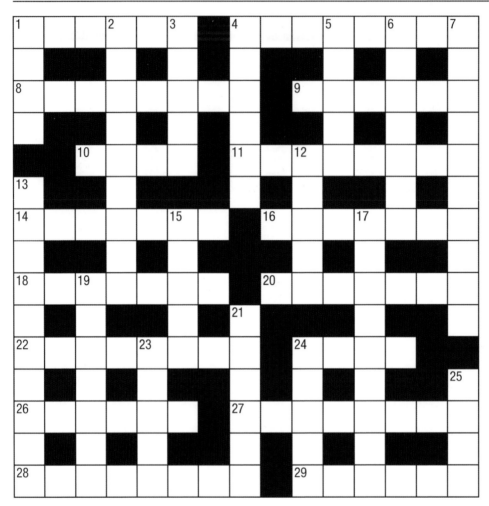

ACROSS
1, 4A Pulped vegetable dish (6, 8)
4 See 1A
8 Team sport with a pitcher and a batter (8)
9 Sentence modifier (6)
10 Principal cook (4)
11 Sacred agreement (8)
14 Commercial goods (7)
16 Having an acrid aroma (7)
18 Italian port near the northeastern border (7)
20 Pupil (7)
22 User (8)
24 Strike open-fisted (4)
26 Embraces, takes on (6)
27 - - - cat, grinning feline (8)
28, 29A Cease to follow the conversation (4, 4, 6)
29 See 28A

DOWN
1 Midnight - - -, Christmas Eve custom (4)
2 Thumb a lift? (9)
3 Red - - -, science fiction sitcom (5)
4 British rock band with the hit Message in a Bottle. The - - - (6)
5 - - - the Giant, iconised French wrestler (5)
6 Perform surgery (7)
7 Proxy (10)
12 Strongroom (5)
13 Eccentric Michael Jackson album? (3, 3, 4)
15 - - - Wainthropp, TV sleuth played by Patricia Routledge (5)
17 The - - -, classic film starring Marlon Brando (9)
19 Ungodly (7)
21 Spring flower (6)
23 Surpass (5)
24 Tabloid (5)
25 Fix (4)

Puzzles

QUIZ 2

1 What countries made up the original Axis powers in World War II?

2 What is "cynophobia"?

3 What is the name of the man who launched eBay back in 1995?

4 What is the common name for dried plums?

5 What was the first feature-length animated movie ever released? (Hint: It was a Disney Movie)

6 Which member of the Beatles married Yoko Ono?

7 Which country borders 14 nations and crosses 8 time zones?

8 What is the loudest animal on Earth?

9 Which country do the cities of Perth, Adelaide and Brisbane belong to?

10 What type of animal is a Flemish giant?

11 Which punctuation mark ends an imperative sentence?

12 Who named the Pacific Ocean?

13 Which country invented ice-cream?

14 What famous US festival hosted over 350,000 fans in 1969?

15 How many hearts does an octopus have?

Were you right? Turn to page 182 for the answers

Who's a clever

When a scruffy mutt turns up on his doorstep, Fred tries his best to turn him away

He was the most unprepossessing dog I'd ever seen. He was grey in colour, hair matted in places, and with brown eyes that gazed at me through a straggly fringe. "Go on! Shoo!" I shouted and waved my walking stick at him.

Unafraid, he sat down a few feet away, tongue lolling in a friendly grin. With some difficulty, I bent down and picked up a ball that had been thrown over the fence by next-door's children. Made of rubber, I knew it wouldn't hurt him but should scare him off.

Big mistake! I aimed it at him, but missed. He bounded off to retrieve it and placed it at my feet, waiting for me to throw it again.

I sighed and stroked his head. He nuzzled my hand. I felt sorry for him and said: "Listen, mate. I don't need a dog. I can barely look after myself." I looked for a collar. His fur was flattened where one had clearly been. He was so thin I was convinced he was a stray or had been abandoned.

Against my better judgement, I gave him some leftover meat which he devoured greedily before trotting off. I hoped it would be the last I saw of him. But the next day he was back in the same place. I hadn't the heart to turn him away so I decided to keep an eye on him, but not let him in the house. My late wife kept the place immaculate and would have been horrified if I'd allowed the scruffy mutt into the living room with its pale beige carpet.

The dog came back every day and gratefully accepted the food I gave him. I even bought some dog biscuits. I suppose the real turning point was when I bought him a collar and started to walk him. Someone had obviously trained him as he behaved well on the lead.

After a few weeks, I began to enjoy our walks. The exercise helped my sore hip and I began to feel in better shape. I was even able to dispense with my walking stick and cut down on my painkillers. My daughter Maria was delighted that I appeared to have a new purpose in life although it was probably only temporary. We both knew that his owner must be looking for him.

One afternoon I gave him a bath and he stood patiently while I soaped him, then carefully hosed him down. Underneath the matted hair I found quite a handsome dog, an Irish wolfhound. Now that he was cleaned up I allowed him into the kitchen where he made himself at home on an old blanket in the corner.

"Someone must be missing you," I told him one morning as I watched him eat his breakfast while I drank my mug of tea.

When she came round for coffee Maria said: "You can't keep him, Dad, although that would be nice. We'll take a photo and put notices on lamp posts and in shop windows. Someone round here must own him."

I agreed with her, but secretly I was hoping that nothing would happen.

As well as putting pictures up locally, she put one on Facebook detailing when and where he was found. Although he was a valuable breed no-one came forward to claim him. To be honest, I was quite relieved.

Then one rainy November evening there was a knock on the door. I opened it to see a petite fair-haired woman peering out from under a hood. "Mr McKenna?" she enquired.

"Yes. Can I help you?"

"I believe you have my dog."

My heart sank as I invited her in. The dog came trotting into the hall. "Jasper!" she exclaimed as he rushed up to her, his tail wagging eagerly. The woman stroked his head.

'Oh well,' I thought to myself. 'It was nice while it lasted'.

The woman told me her name was Jackie and said: "I really don't know how he got here. We live over a hundred miles away. He'd been to the vet for a check-up and before I could put his collar back on a

> "You can't keep him, Dad, although that would be nice. We'll put notices on lamp posts"

BY VAL ROBERTS

dog?

lorry thundered past and he ran off." Her eyes filled with tears.

I said: "No wonder he looked so bedraggled."

Jackie went on: "He's a lovely natured dog, but we have to re-home him as my husband has a new job in America."

The dog came and sat by my side. He looked up at me and I said: "So your name is Jasper, is it?" Gently taking him by the collar, I returned him to Jackie. Jasper licked her hand then, ducking his head apologetically, he walked back to me.

She laughed. "It looks like he has found a new owner all by himself. Who's a clever dog then?"

Jasper wagged his tail and gave a wide grin as though he knew the answer to that perennial question. Yes, of course he was a clever dog.

Twenty-one today

*Writer Marion Clarke and **Yours** readers recall how we celebrated coming of age*

I hope you like this photo (above) of me on my 21st birthday with the beautiful cake my mother made and pink roses sent by my boyfriend. Among my presents were – somewhat bizarrely – a set of silver-plated 'apostle' teaspoons and the complete works of Shakespeare!

Valerie Reilly also received a rather unusual present when she came of age. "My parents hired a room above a pub for a large party. We had a three-piece band playing and Mum had ordered a big iced cake with my name on top. My parents gave me a watch and I also had several plastic 'silver' keys. My gifts were displayed on a table which was a bit embarrassing as my husband got me a pink electric ladies' shaver in a leather box!"

Now in her 90s, **Joyce Dickins** says her family didn't have much money to spend on celebrations, but she still wears the brooch her parents gave her. "I was given £1 for my birthday and my mother went to the pawn shop and bought me a secondhand brooch. It has been

through the washing machine over and over again and still comes out as bright as the day I was 21."

Times were still hard when **Adrienne Winkley** came of age in 1946; the war was just over and she was in the Auxiliary Territorial Service (ATS). "I had a few hours off on my birthday. I managed to get some transport to go and see my mum. I was nearly in tears when she gave me a little cake she'd made with ingredients saved from her rations. There was a piece of white paper on top (no icing!) and she had cut out the numbers two and one from cardboard and covered them with silver paper from a cigarette packet."

Jill Hassall was just a baby in the year that Adrienne was 21 and in 1957 the council in Newport, Monmouthshire, held a 'Welcome to Citizenship' evening for everyone born in 1946. "I was one of the post-war Boom Babies and there were so many of us they had to host two separate occasions!"

Elizabeth Jameson had been married for seven months when her birthday came around. "My husband gave me a large present. It was too big for jewellery and I wondered what it could be. I unwrapped it and found it was a canteen of cutlery.

I was lost for words! 42 years later I still have the cutlery – and the husband!"

Her birthday in July 1953 was just another working day for **Sheila Smith.** "I was on duty as a staff nurse on a busy female surgical ward. I was trying to do the ladies' dressings when an auxiliary nurse came up to me with a bouquet. I thought it was for a patient and asked her to deal with the flowers herself. However, the bouquet was for me – 21 red roses from a very special auntie."

Sheila didn't miss out because she had a party for friends and relatives at a church hall the following evening.

Anne Holcroft's big birthday also found her in hospital, but for a different reason. "My son was born – two weeks late – in the early hours of my 21st birthday. When one of the nurses saw my cards she got the whole ward (20 new mums) and the staff to sing Happy Birthday to me. At least my son has no excuse to forget my birthday!"

Jill Larter quite literally got the key of the door when she came of age on January 30, 1960. "I collected the keys for our newly built house on my special day."

Sheila Joyce has a similar tale to tell: "We had just got our first home which badly needed decorating. I spent my 21st painting, wallpapering and

cleaning. It was certainly a memorable day."

When she was 21 in May 1961 **Jacqueline Harris** was treading the boards at the Chanticleer Theatre in London. "I was in a group of amateur actors called The Cicala Players. We were all employees of Martins Bank and appearing in a play called The Master Key.

"I thought that the cast and backstage staff had forgotten it was my special day, but after the final curtain a huge silver key, signed by everybody, a beautiful bouquet of flowers plus a birthday cake were brought on the stage to the delight of the audience. I was thrilled."

On the day that she reached the age of consent in 1950, **Stephanie Evans** got engaged. "In the morning we went together to buy my ring, a sparkly diamond. In the evening, there was a sit-down meal for family and friends in a local hall, with dancing afterwards.

"At about 11.30pm someone reminded us that it was the last night of the St Peter's fair which was held every year in the market square in Holsworthy and said, 'We can catch the last rides'. So off went all the younger ones, including the engaged couple, and we had a great end to my lovely day. It was pouring with rain, but who cared!"

Betty Woodruff had two 21st birthdays, celebrating the second one with her daughter, son-in-law, grandchildren and great grand-daughter... 1928 was a leap year!

Put your glad rags

Louise would rather stay at home watching a film than go to the pub quiz

BY SUSAN WRIGHT

I don't often get unexpected visitors so I was alarmed when my doorbell rang one evening. Alarmed, and rather irritated, I paused the film I was watching and went to the door in case it was something urgent.

"Hi!" my sister Sarah said as I peered through the narrow gap. "Put your glad rags on – we're going out tonight."

"I'm not going anywhere," I replied, taking the chain off the door.

"Oh, yes you are!" Sarah said. "You're going to a pub quiz."

"Since when?" I asked, wondering if I'd forgotten about this arrangement.

"Since now. They are having a quiz night at the Royal Oak and we need one more person to make up our team."

"But I'm watching a really good film," I protested.

Sarah grinned. "Yes, I guessed you would be. Is it You've Got Mail or The Holiday for the umpteenth time?"

"Neither. It's Serendipity."

"Oh, is that the one with the gloves?"

"Yes, the one with the gloves and John Cusack and New York," I agreed as I led the way into the living-room. "And it's only just started."

My sister glanced at the television. "You can watch it any night of the week, but the quiz is one night only and there will be mulled wine and mince pies."

end with 'happily ever after' and you are on your own now because your marriage didn't end that way," Sarah said with brutal honesty.

"That's true, but we were really happy before it all went wrong," I said, welling up at the memory of the good times we'd had before I'd split up with my ex.

"Hey, don't cry, sis. We were all fond of James, but it's time you moved on." She looked at her watch. "Now you need to go and get changed or we'll be late."

I looked down at my comfy old onesie: "Do I have to?"

"Yes, you do!" she laughed. "Come on, Louise, it's going to be more fun than sitting at home

---

"Get your skates on, Fred will be wondering where we are!"

---

drooling over John Cusack."

I relented because I knew how stubborn Sarah can be. "What shall I wear?"

"Your glad rags! How about a smart pair of trousers and a sparkly top? After all, it's nearly Christmas."

I asked: "Is it just going to be the three of us? You, Fred and me?"

"No, we need four to make up a team. Now for Heaven's sake get your skates on, Fred will be wondering where we are!"

I couldn't understand why she was in such a hurry, but it all made sense when we walked into the Royal Oak and I saw who was sitting at our table with my brother-in-law.

"James!" I gasped, my heart thumping.

My ex smiled. "Hi, Louise. How are you? You're looking great."

"Thanks," I stammered, staring at him in disbelief.

"And I've brought you a little present," he said, handing me

a beautifully wrapped box as I collapsed onto a chair.

"Can I open it now?"

"Of course."

I ripped the paper off to find a box of my favourite chocolates.

James grinned. "I thought you'd enjoy eating them while you are watching your favourite romcoms."

"Oh, I will," I said, gazing into his sparkling blue eyes and realising I was still madly in love with him. "I'm afraid I didn't bring you anything as I had no idea you'd be here."

"Do you mind that I'm here?"

I shook my head. "No, I don't mind, but I didn't even know that you were back in this country."

James looked over at my sister who was trying to assume an innocent expression. He said: "I thought it would be a wise move to get in touch with Sarah first. I needed to check out the lie of the land."

"And?"

"She reckoned you'd be happy to see me and assured me you weren't dating anyone else. Are you? Happy, I mean?"

I nodded. "Yes, both happy to see you and definitely not dating anyone."

"That's a relief. I've missed you so much, Louise, and I think we made a big mistake."

"What sort of big mistake?"

"I believe we gave up on our marriage too soon." He paused as a barmaid arrived with a plate of mince pies which she put down on the table. "I've given it a lot of thought and I think we should try again."

"Oh, so do I!" I breathed, thinking how stupid I'd been to insist I didn't want to go out because I was watching Serendipity.

Across the table, my sister winked at me. "Glad you came now?" she asked, raising her glass of mulled wine in a toast to the two of us.

I sighed as I sank down on the sofa. "This is my favourite romcom."

"But you can watch it any time you want."

"Yes, but I'm in the mood to watch it now," I insisted. "It's the best Christmas film ever."

Sarah said: "I don't understand why you are so obsessed with these romcoms. I would have thought they'd just make you sad."

"Why?"

"Well, because they all

QUICK CROSSWORD 3

ACROSS
1 Peak (6)
4 John - - -, veteran journalist and regular on The One Show (8)
8 Distressed, frantic (2, 1, 5)
9 Rock - - -, Fifties and Sixties film star (6)
10 Buttress (4)
11 Calm endurance (8)
14 Incessant talker (7)
16 Accumulate (7)
18 Dyed and seasoned English sausage (7)
20 Captain Jack - - -, Johnny Depp's buccaneer (7)
22 Rascal (8)
24 Weighty book (4)
26 Farmyard feedbox (6)
27 Expressing (views) indirectly (8)
28 Wavering (8)
29 Astute (6)

DOWN
1 Rouse, awaken (4)
2 Dejected (9)
3 Vagrant (5)
4 The Legend of - - - Hollow, novella by Washington Irving (6)
5 Antoni - - -, designer of Barcelona's Sagrada Família (5)
6 - - - makes the heart grow fonder, saying (7)
7 Hollywood's nickname (10)
12 Cavalry unit (5)
13 Peevish individual (10)
15 Eldest son of Cain (5)
17 Local dignitary (4, 5)
19 Assorted (7)
21 The - - -, 2011 Oscar-winning silent film with James Cromwell (6)
23 Vision (5)
24 Appetisers in Spanish cuisine (5)
25 Advanced in years (4)

QUIZ 3

1 How many languages are written from right to left?

2 Who was the first woman to win a Nobel Prize in 1903?

3 What is the name given to Indian food cooked over charcoal in a clay oven?

4 What were the four main characters' names in the TV series "Golden Girls" that ran from 1985-1992?

5 Area 51 is located in which US state?

6 Which was the first soft drink in space?

7 Which is the smallest country in the world?

8 What are the folds of skin on a cat's ears called?

9 What is the name of the biggest technology company in South Korea?

10 From which country does Gouda cheese originate?

11 Which country in the world has the most natural lakes?

12 When Walt Disney was a child, which character did he play at school?

13 What is a group of ravens known as?

14 Which mammals lay eggs?

15 Who wrote the first dictionary?

Were you right? Turn to page 182 for the answers

Sangria and castanets

The sound of flamenco music evokes memories of Julie's long ago holiday romance

Thursday night is flamenco night. I take time to prepare – my dress is very old; I bought it from a shop down a backstreet in Marbella and it cost a fortune. The bodice is red and it contrasts with the ruffles of the skirt which are black with gold polka dots.

It's a real squeeze fitting into it. Every time I'm tempted to eat a chocolate éclair, I remind myself how tight this dress is.

I oil my jet-black hair and pull it back into a bun. I dye it – if I didn't it would be grey. My hairdresser has suggested toning it down with low lights. She says it's kinder to older skintones, but I like it black. I used to have a mantilla, but the moths got it. Instead, I pin a white artificial rose behind my ear that I bought at the market.

I start putting on my make-up. I use a dark foundation as I want to look suntanned, but it sinks into my wrinkles. I apply eyeliner, lashings of mascara and I use gel to create eyebrows where mine used to be. I finish with scarlet lipstick, remembering a time when my lips were plump and kissable. I know I've overdone my make-up, but it's fun.

Next I put on a pair of black Mary Jane shoes in an extra-wide fitting. The proper flamenco ones are too uncomfortable these days and anyway the nails in the soles would ruin the lounge floor. Also, the noise would be deafening and Queenie next door already whinges about flamenco night. I study myself in the mirror and I like what I see. I'm ready to dance.

In the kitchen, I pour two glasses of sangria and take a sip. I hate drinking on my own. The other glass remains untouched as I heat the tapas from the supermarket. Patatas bravas, meatballs, spicy prawns and ham croquetas.

I select a record – The Best of Flamenco 1979 (Various Artists) – which I bought at a car boot sale. I take a plastic flower from the vase on the sideboard and clamp the stem firmly between my teeth. Then I dance in time to the music, concentrating on my foot movements; toe, heel, heel, toe, flat. When the music stops I shout "Olé!" and the plastic flower drops to the floor.

I look at the photograph of Pedro, taken in Lloret de Mar in 1977. The year I met him. My friend Kathy and I went there on a bargain holiday. Twelve days by coach! We stayed in a two-star hotel with hard beds and no hot water. Back then, I thought the food was horrible, all garlic and oil. It gave me indigestion.

But Lloret felt like paradise – the sunshine, swimming in the warm sea and Cava at 50p a bottle. Pedro was one of the waiters. He had a mop of black curly hair and come-to-bed brown eyes. It was a holiday romance and my first real boyfriend.

BY BARBARA COMPTON

"I bought a straw donkey... but that was not the only thing I brought home with me"

The music changes. I pick up my black lace fan. I've had it a long time and there is a small tear in it now; it is a bit battered. I wave it around seductively to the sound of a guitar. I draw the fan across my cheek – that means 'I love you'. Then I swing it behind my head. That means 'Don't forget me'.

As I twirl the fan around, I keep my eyes on another photo of Pedro. He is standing behind an enormous dish of paella – it was taken on the Spanish night the hotel held on the last day of our holiday. The entertainment included a demonstration of flamenco dancing. When they asked the guests to have a go, I was the first one in the queue. Pedro taught me the basic steps and we danced until dawn.

I cried when I left Lloret de Mar. I bought a large straw donkey to take back to England. That was not the only thing I brought home with me. Four weeks later, I discovered I was pregnant.

It's time for another dance. This time I use my castanets, made of black hardwood. There used to be a Spanish flag painted on each one but that has worn away over the years. The one in my right hand makes a low-pitched noise while the one in my left hand is high-pitched. I click away. My son Marco loved to hear their clatter when he was a toddler. He's in his 40s now and every bit as handsome as his father. There is a lovely photo of him on the mantelpiece.

The doorbell rings just as I am enjoying myself. I hope it isn't Queenie coming round to complain about the noise again. I don't want to stop now but I have to open the door.

"I forgot my key, Jools. I see you've started without me."

His hair is grey, but his eyes still twinkle in a way that makes my heart flutter. It's Pedro.

Hippies, mods and

Writer Marion Clarke and **Yours** *readers share memories of their teenage lifestyles*

Never do our music and clothes say so much about us than when we are teenagers. My teenage years coincided with the birth of rock 'n' roll and I still love the singers I first heard on Radio Luxembourg – Fats Domino, Sam Cooke and Elvis – although I long ago stopped wearing starched petticoats under a full skirt cinched in with a wide belt!

Rosemary Medland grew up in the same era: "My big sister, her best friend and I used to bike more than three miles to the next village where there was a milk bar. We all wore net petticoats under our floral skirts teamed with fluorescent ankle socks in pink or green.

"My sister's friend gave me some money for the juke box and as we were all in love with Elvis, I chose Let Me Be Your Teddy Bear. We used to jive with some young servicemen

and had lots of laughs trying to keep in step with the tempo."

A decade later, **Liz Shaw** grew up in the age of flower power: "I became a hippie in the Sixties when my older brother took me to Donovan concerts. We also went to the Windsor jazz and blues festival where I was lifted onto people's shoulders so I could see the stage.

"I wore brightly coloured kaftans made of cheesecloth or velvet. I loved my stripey shirt and floral trousers which I wore together and was most upset when a neighbour commented that I was wearing pyjamas! The perfume of the time was patchouli oil which was very strong and musky."

Liz completed her outfits with beads, a jangling bell necklace and her 'make love not war' badge.

Elaine Jacklin also loved Donovan as well as Bob Dylan and Joan Baez: "I desperately wanted to be a hippy. I had a purple flowered dress that I wore with long strings of beads and a bell. When I wore this to work, someone complained about the tinkling of the bell! I also had

rockers

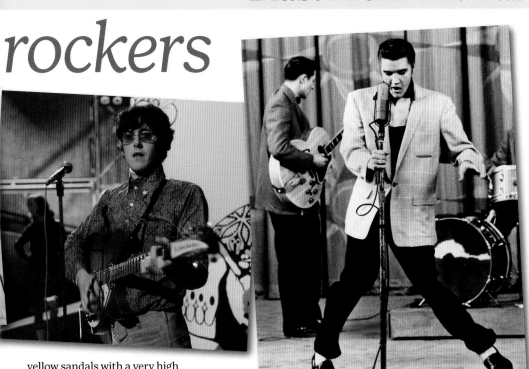

yellow sandals with a very high cork wedge. People used to ask me how I managed to walk in those sandals. When I look at the flat, sensible shoes I wear now I also wonder how I did it."

While hippies drifted around in floaty kaftans with flowers in their hair, dreaming of going to San Francisco, mods rode Vespa or Lambretta scooters, wore parkas and were more likely to dream of going to Brighton.

Sylvia Foster writes:
"I was a mod and hung about with the scooter boys we met in milk bars or coffee houses. We used to go to a local club where we danced to music by The Hollies and The Beatles. My parents wouldn't have been happy if they'd known we were in the club, not the coffee house!

"Hot pants were all the rage and we also wore short shift dresses with white pull-on plastic boots."

Marjorie Edwards was a mod, too, and on Friday nights she used to hang around the ITV studios in Holborn where they recorded Ready, Steady, Go!
"We screamed the place down when pop stars came in or out

of the building. Once we found the door left open so we crept in and tiptoed along the corridors and walked straight into Gene Pitney of Twenty-Four Hours from Tulsa fame. He had just come off stage and he was sweaty and his fake tan make-up was running down his face, but he was still gorgeous!"

Marjorie once caught a glimpse of The Beatles, but for her the highlight was once again sneaking in through the stage door and meeting Billy J Kramer and the Dakotas. "I adored Billy J and said, 'Oh, please give me a kiss!' – he gave me a quick peck on the cheek. I've never forgotten that!"

While Elaine was swooning over the pop stars of the day, **Ann Rowe** was dancing the night away at clubs such as The Flamingo in Wardour Street in Soho. "We used to go to clubs that played soul music by artists like Otis Redding and Wilson Pickett.

"I think my parents despaired

when I went off to places like Brighton and Margate on Bank Holidays. They were exhausting weekends when we danced all night and tried to sleep on the beach during the day! The early evenings would find all the public toilets filled with mod girls getting washed and changed for another night's clubbing. They were really fun times!"

Whether we were hippies, mods or rockers, our parents despaired of our clothes.
Gaynor Waters thought she looked great in her lace-up Hush Puppy shoes worn with a thin nylon navy mac: "Despite my mother telling me I'd freeze to death, this was my uniform for going out – but I was terribly cold during the winter months!"

Sheila Peters used to make her own clothes: "I liked to copy Mary Quant designs, especially colour-block dresses. My skirts got shorter and shorter and Mum used to tut, 'That's not a skirt, it's a pelmet!'

Setting sail again

Newly widowed Ellie feels lost in the big old house where she brought up her family

Ellie hesitated before turning off the radio on her bedside table, knowing the silence would deepen her loneliness.

She'd considered switching to a classical music channel at night, but that meant she'd miss the shipping forecast. Since Jim had died she'd come to rely on the familiar music of Sailing By to lull her to sleep. The announcer's calm voice was a signal for her brain to switch off and allow her to relax.

When her husband had been in hospital she had rarely turned on the radio even though she was alone in the house they had bought after their first son was born. But after he'd gone she found she depended on the sound of voices to keep her company.

Her thoughts returned to that sad time. The words of the poem, 'Do not go gentle into that good night' haunted her. She wished that Jim had been able to 'go gentle'.

Every evening when she left the ward she used to say goodnight to him as he lay perfectly still with his eyes closed. And she told him that he could let go just as soon as he felt ready. Ellie was careful never to say: "See you tomorrow, darling" in case it encouraged him to hang on for another day. She worried that he was clinging on for her sake, not wanting her to be left alone.

On arriving home, she dealt with all the messages left on her phone. She knew that her family and friends were trying to show their support, but all she wanted at that stage was to get a cup of tea and a piece of toast and watch something undemanding on television. She was too exhausted to put on a brave front.

Ellie recalled one night in particular when she had been watching some daft comedy to take her mind off things. She had begun by chuckling, but her laughter turned suddenly to tears and she found herself weeping helplessly, great gulping sobs. Tears ran unchecked down her cheeks.

She knew that thanks to medication Jim would be sleeping peacefully, but that evening she wept for herself, for the years gone by and the years still to come. She was crying for the girl she had been, the young woman becoming a mother who had often resented the years of dreary housework. Jim had been proud to be the breadwinner, believing she enjoyed being at home with the children – and she had, but she also wished for more independence.

Turning the television off, she'd retreated to bed. After tossing and turning, she switched on the radio to hear the familiar music of Sailing By and eventually drifted off to the soothing sound of the sea. She slept soundly only to be woken by the strident ringing of the phone. It was the call from the hospital that Ellie had half hoped for and half dreaded.

The following weeks had been incredibly busy with people coming and going and the funeral to arrange. Jim's old schoolfriend who had been best man at their wedding gave the eulogy. Ellie read Afterwards by Thomas Hardy, a poem that she and Jim had both loved and now took on a deeper meaning.

Once the funeral was over, there had been far too much time on her hands. Sometimes Ellie wondered if being widowed at 50 was harder than being divorced. Listening to friends who had been unceremoniously dumped for a younger model, she decided that maybe it was.

Instead of online dating, she did voluntary work at the local food bank. She loved having the grandchildren to stay in the school holidays, but as time went by the big roomy house had felt emptier than ever.

One spring morning, Ellie woke with a start and the sense of a new beginning. It was time she moved on. Literally! She made herself a mug of tea, opened up her laptop and searched the property websites for flats. Having satisfied herself that they were very affordable for someone with a spacious

BY PENNY GLENDAY

"One morning, Ellie woke with the sense of a new beginning. It was time to move on"

family house to sell, she got dressed and started work.

She took out a roll of bin bags and began with the airing cupboard, keeping only the newest sheets and fluffiest towels. From there she went to the bookshelves. She filled a box with Jim's collection of history books and thrillers by John Grisham.

The next day she started on the wardrobes. In addition to many of her own clothes that she hadn't worn for years, she added to the pile Jim's favourite old gardening jacket which she couldn't bear to part with until now. By the time she'd finished she had six bulging bags to take to the charity shop.

A year later Ellie was settled in her comfortable flat overlooking the park and within walking distance of the town centre. With the buzz of life going on all around her she no longer needed the voices on the radio to keep her company, but she still listened to the shipping forecast as she drifted off to sleep every night.

QUICK CROSSWORD 4

ACROSS
1 Portion of a circle or pie chart (6)
4 Meaty hotpot (4, 4)
9 Horizontal-bar exercise (4-2)
10 Intense dislike (8)
12 The - - - King, popular musical (4)
13 Girder (5)
14 Labyrinth (4)
17 Smart attire (7, 5)
20 Theatre hand busy between acts (5, 7)
23 Capital of the Lazio region (4)
24 Common viper (5)
25 Crowd together (4)
28 Speckled garden bird (8)
29, 6D One-way ticket (6, 4)
30 Reduced by editing (8)
31 See-in-the-dark vegetable? (6)

DOWN
1 Company's source of goods (8)
2 Folded pizzas (8)
3 Musical composition (4)
5 King of Rock 'n' Roll (5, 7)
6 See 29 Across
7 Displaying loyalty to a group (6)
8 - - - poster, trope of westerns (6)
11 Bother, commotion (4, 3, 5)
15 Nip (5)
16 Meaty jelly (5)
18 The - - -, 1977 album by Billy Joel (8)
19 Extensive view (8)
21 Swiss toboggan run (6)
22 Hinder (6)
26 Clump of dirt (4)
27 Passport stamp (4)

Puzzles

QUIZ 4

1 How many countries still have Shilling as currency?

2 What is the name of the largest ocean on earth?

3 Hendrick's, Larios and Seagram's are some of the best-selling brands of which spirit?

4 What is the biggest-selling music single of all time?

5 Demolition of the Berlin wall separating East and West Germany began in what year?

6 Who created Sherlock Holmes?

7 In which country would you find Lake Bled?

8 How long do elephant pregnancies last?

9 What is the Romanised Arabic word for "moon"?

10 Which TV series showed the first interracial kiss on American network television?

11 Havana is the capital of what country?

12 What is the hottest planet in the solar system?

13 Who invented the word "vomit"?

14 How many legs does a spider have?

15 Which tissues connect the muscles to the bones?

Were you right? Turn to page 182 for the answers

ith **Yours** 2023   175

Down all the years

BY SHARON HASTON

Carol is dreading her big birthday – how can life have flown by so quickly?

As I chopped the veg for the stir-fry, I sighed: "I can't believe I'm going to be fifty."

"Well, there's not much you can do about it," Dan said, putting his arms around me.

"Promise me this – no surprise party, no cake and definitely no candles! I'm going to go to bed and hide under the duvet."

Dan laughed: "Okay! Okay!

But seriously, you've achieved a lot in those fifty years, Carol. You should celebrate that."

I stared glumly out of the window at a finch perched in the apple tree. I enjoyed my job and I loved Dan and our daughter Louise, but this big birthday had me thinking there must be more to life…Some unknown adventure I'd missed out on.

The next day I felt restless.

Dan was at football and Louise was shopping with friends. I opened my wardrobe door to see if I had anything to wear in case I changed my mind about having a party. I'd put on some weight so maybe a revamp of my wardrobe would cheer me up.

As I rifled disconsolately through my dresses, I noticed our old photo albums on the top shelf. I lifted them down and sat on the floor to

Dad had with a separate flash cube that was attached for night-time photos.

By the time he'd taken pictures of my sixth birthday party he'd bought an Instamatic. I smiled at the one of me blowing out the candles on my cake. Things were simpler in those days. Our party food was cheese-and-pickle sandwiches followed by jelly and ice cream. Afterwards we played games like Pass the Parcel and Musical Chairs and admired Dad's photos as they whizzed out of the Instamatic.

On Christmas Day, I was pictured in my pyjamas sitting astride my new bike and holding up my Twinkle annual. And there were Nana and Grandpa in paper hats looking on as Mum held up the Christmas pudding.

For our first holiday abroad, Dad invested in a more compact camera and I'd been allowed to take the photo of him and Mum standing outside a beautiful whitewashed church in bright sunshine. They looked tanned and happy.

The photos of my school leaving dance were taken with the camera I'd been given for my eighteenth birthday. I must have used a whole can of mousse on my curly perm! We danced under coloured disco lights to music played by a DJ on vinyl records. My Louise wouldn't have a clue what vinyl was!

And there was Dan with his floppy brown hair and flared jeans. We had started dating around the time this photo was taken. How on earth had we gone from happy-go-lucky teenagers to responsible adults in what seemed like the blink of an eye?

The next album had photos of me at my graduation, looking self-conscious in a gown and mortarboard, clutching a scroll in one hand.

Dan had teased me because I was terrified I might trip up when crossing the stage to be presented with my degree.

Ah! Our honeymoon at Lake Bled. There was a postcard of the monastery on the island where Dan had followed the tradition for newlyweds by carrying me up its ninety-eight steps. Unfortunately, we forgot to pack a camera and bought a cheap plastic one at the airport so there were lots of photos where the tops of our heads are missing or shots showing nothing but blue sky.

As time passed the photos in the albums changed to ones of beautiful scenery taken on various holidays. Dan bought me an advanced photo system camera with a panorama setting which produced long rectangular photos.

We took that camera with us to San Francisco where we went to celebrate Dan's fortieth birthday. When we asked a passer-by to take a shot of the three of us standing by the Golden Gate bridge, we had to instruct her how to use it.

Not long after that, we went digital and now, like everyone else, we use our mobiles to take photos so they are stored on our computers instead of in albums.

I hugged the albums to me. Everyone I loved was captured forever in those pages, bringing back precious memories. Looking through them made me realise that my life had been full of adventures and happy times.

I stood up and put the albums back in the wardrobe. Being fifty really wasn't so bad. I had loads more memories to make. I was going to celebrate with a proper party for family friends and take lots of photos to treasure in the years to come.

"This birthday had me thinking there must be more to life"

browse through them. Flicking through the first one I came across my baby photos, most of them in black and white. Mum and Dad had splashed out on a colour film for my christening. Mum looked radiant in her pink dress and matching jacket, beaming proudly with me in her arms.

There were holiday snaps of me riding a donkey and building a sandcastle on the beach at Blackpool. I remembered the bulky camera

Dear Santa

Yours *writer Marion Clarke and* **Yours** *readers recall the thrill of Christmas when we still believed in Santa*

I still have my first letter to Santa which I wrote when I was four. The handwriting is my father's so I must have dictated it to him. Among my requests are a blue handkerchief for my dolls and a fairy for the Christmas tree. Concerned about his risky descent down the chimney, I reassured Santa that the fire would not be lit on Christmas Eve!

Wilma Hart followed tradition by putting her letter to Santa up the chimney. "Later that evening, our neighbour came in to see us and I told her about my letter. She said, 'That must have been what I saw fluttering on your chimney top as I came along the street'. I was very excited that she had

actually seen it and, hopefully, so would Santa."

Teresa Campbell remembers the thrill of believing in Father Christmas as well as the disillusion later. "The eager anticipation and preparations – leaving out a carrot for the reindeer and a drink and mince pie for Santa – then coming down the next morning to see if they had gone were probably even more magical than the gifts."

But her faith was shattered when she went to a Christmas bazaar. "A man we knew had taken on the role of Santa and my friend's cousin suddenly exclaimed, 'Santa, don't you own the pub across the road?'"

It was **Jo Minett's** grandfather who accidentally

gave the game away when she was a little girl. "Santa had come and I dived into my sack and pulled out a doll, beautifully dressed in a knitted blue matinee jacket and trousers with a spare yellow dress and a white cape, only to hear my sleepy granddad say to my nan, 'Aren't they the dollies' clothes you knitted, Betsy?' Christmas was never the same again!"

Our high hopes of Santa were all too often dashed, as **Sharron Radford** recalls. "I desperately wanted a Sindy doll and put her at the top of my list. When the big day came I was deeply disappointed that I did not get her. Instead I got a huge doll that 'talked' when you pulled a cord in her back. My dad tried to

Dear Santa Claus,...

convince me that her name was Sandy and she was Sindy's older sister. I was not impressed!"

It was a shiny new bike that **Margaret Rymer** longed for. "My granddad said he would see what he could do. I was beside myself with excitement. On Christmas morning I came downstairs to find my granddad's heavy old black bicycle in the living room. I was shocked, but pleased that at least it was a bike – and he did eventually get me a better one when I learned to ride it. Even that one was second-hand, but I was happy nonetheless."

Like most of us, **Ann Swain** was blissfully ignorant of the pressure on our parents who often struggled to find the right present. "When I was six I asked for a twin dolls' pram. When I eagerly dashed downstairs on Christmas morning, there was a beautiful Silver Cross pram with my favourite doll, Rosemary, looking very pretty in new clothes, all made by my mum. But it wasn't a twin one!

"Years later I discovered that after weeks of being upset with herself for not being able to fulfil my dream, she had come across an advert for a second-hand pram which had a dent in it. Mum told me the dent happened as Santa struggled to get it down the chimney.

"I cherished that pram until I was 24 when I moved into a tiny flat and reluctantly gave it away to charity."

Jean Gee grew up in the war and toys were scarce. When she was five, her family escaped from bombed-out London to rural Essex where a children's party was held in the squire's barn. "There was a huge Christmas tree supplied from his estate and the local ladies had made sure there was a present on it for every child.

"I spotted a teddy bear and hoped he would be my present. He was 'preloved' of course and a lady who was handy with her needle had used flowered material to hide the wear and tear to his ears, paws and feet. He sported a tie in the same material.

"To my delight, he was handed to me! He became my dearest toy for many years."

Sadly, Jean's beloved teddy was lost when they moved house, but **Elizabeth Richards** nearly lost hers in a different way. She and her family lived in a freezing farmhouse so she asked Santa for a warm blanket and a hot water bottle as well as a teddy. But, as they were opening their presents, disaster struck. "Mum said she could smell burning and rushed out of bed to find the electric heater was sparking and a cloth had caught fire. My dad got the flames under control, but I kept sobbing that all my presents would be burned.

"Mum soothed me with a big hug and made us all hot chocolate, then we resumed unwrapping our presents. I still have my teddy bear which I named Andrew. All my grandchildren are allowed a cuddle but they are not allowed to play with him!"

To Santa xxx

What's app, Alec?

Buying her husband a smartphone has an unpredicted outcome for Val

> **"Today alone he'd bombarded her with three photos of a badly parked car…"**

BY JULIA PAILLIER

"Someone loves you!" said Dee as Val's phone pinged for the umpteenth time since she'd entered the salon.

Val rolled her eyes. "Someone got a smartphone for his birthday."

"Aw, sweet! One of the grandkids?"

"No, a much bigger kid, and I'm beginning to regret giving it to him."

Buying her husband Alec a new phone for his birthday had been Val's way of nudging him into the digital age. He had kept his ancient pay-as-you-go phone shut in the glove compartment of his car, only to be used in an emergency.

But her plan had backfired. Alec had taken to the wonders of the latest technology with more enthusiasm than she'd expected. Today alone he'd bombarded her with six photos of a squirrel attempting to get at the nuts in their bird feeder, three of a badly parked car in the street, and one selfie.

And she'd lost count of the number of texts he'd sent, complete with emojis and

Short story

annoying abbreviations such as 'pizza 2nite?' and 'c u L8r'.

Evenings spent chatting or watching a film together were a thing of the past. Alec was glued to the online gardening forum or the community Facebook page.

"I'm home!" she called, dropping her keys on the hall table.

Alec was sitting on the sofa, focused on his mobile.

"I've been to the hairdresser's," Val said, waiting for his usual appreciative comment.

"This Wordle is a really tough one," he grunted without taking his eyes from the screen.

When they met for their regular Thursday morning coffee, her daughter Emma laughed: "Don't worry, Mum, Dad has always had these fads. Remember the Spanish lessons when he drove us mad with all the 'holas' and dreams of starting a fish-and-chip shop in Benidorm?"

Val joined in: "And the DIY phase when he sanded down every piece of furniture and painted it. Your Nan had a fit when she saw the oak bookcase she gave us for a wedding present transformed into shabby chic!"

They both collapsed into giggles.

Val's expression grew serious: "It's hard to see the funny side of this fad, Em. We hardly talk these days – we just text each other. He's always tapping away at his blinking phone. Honestly, it's worse than another woman!"

Emma nodded. "The twins loved Granddad being online, but even they are getting fed up with his constant video calls. You've got to do something about

it, Mum."

"I agree, but what? Accidentally drop the wretched thing out of an upstairs window? He would just go out and buy a replacement."

"You need to come up with a distraction," Emma mused. "Look at the pattern up to now. Dad is always carried away with his latest hobby until the next one comes along."

Two days later, Val was convinced she'd come up with the perfect plan.

"What's this?" Alec asked, picking up the leaflet she had left lying on the kitchen table.

"It was posted though the door," Val said casually. "Something about a fitness class at the community centre. Put it in the recycling."

"First ten sessions are half price. Not bad," Alex went on.

Val said: "Hmm. Not for the fainthearted, though. The instructor's ex-army."

A lec turned the leaflet over. "Guaranteed to build strength, stamina and cardio health," he read out loud. "You know, I might give this a go. I've tried some of the exercise stuff on YouTube, but it's not the same as being in a group. I could do with losing this spare tyre. You too, love, if I'm honest. What about it?"

Val gulped. She hadn't expected that. She'd have to dig out her leggings and go along

to the first session for moral support, but it would be worth it to wean Alec off is mobile.

"So how are the bootcamp sessions coming along?" Emma asked a few weeks later.

"I've lost three pounds."

"You look fantastic, Mum. You're even moving differently."

"I only went to keep your dad company, but I'm hooked. Last night he treated me to dinner at that new vegetarian restaurant."

"You mean Dad has actually given up steak and kidney pud?" Emma said in disbelief.

"We've started to see fitness as a lifestyle choice, Em," Val explained.

"But is he spending less time on his phone?"

"Well..." Val stopped as Alec burst into the kitchen, puffing like a steam engine."

"Halfway to my ten thousand target," he crowed, fishing his phone from his pocket.

"Ten thousand what?" Emma asked, baffled.

"Steps! I've downloaded this brilliant app that counts them for you. Mum has it on her phone as well."

Val nodded sheepishly. "Er, coffee, love?"

"No, mineral water," Alec took a bottle from the fridge. "We've got diet apps, too, with meal planners to make sure we get the right balance of fats and protein."

Emma raised her eyebrows. "Wow – the marvels of modern technology!"

"I had no idea before your mum gave me this phone," Alec grinned, planting an affectionate kiss on Val's cheek. "Only someone who knows me really well could have chosen such a perfect present."

Puzzle answers

QUICK CROSSWORD NO.1

Page 150
ACROSS
1 Plaice, 4 Scrabble, 9 Easels, 10 Au revoir,
12 Eyre, 13 Coach, 14 Burn, 17 Victoria Wood,
20 Collared dove, 23 Adam, 24 Yokel,
25 Team, 28 Helsinki, 29 Lagoon, 30 Rosemary,
31 Adonis.
DOWN
1 Preserve, 2 Abstract, 3 Colt, 5 Churchwarden,
6 Apex, 7 Brogue, 8 Errand, 11 Social worker,
15 Colon, 16 Noddy, 18 Comedown, 19 Terminus,
21 Father, 22 Dallas, 26 Firm, 27 Laud.

QUIZ NO.1

Page 151
1. World Wide Web. 2. Octagon. 3. Horse.
4. Switzerland. 5. Mr Potato Head. 6. Anastasia
and Drizella. 7. India. 8. Amelia Earhart. 9. Honey.
10. Scotland. 11. Henry VIII. 12. Hippopotamus.
13. 50m. 14. Brown. 15. Tea.

QUICK CROSSWORD NO.2

Page 158
ACROSS
1 Mashed, 4 Potatoes, 8 Softball, 9 Adverb,
10 Chef, 11 Covenant, 14 Freight,
16 Pungent, 18 Trieste, 20 Student,
22 Employer, 24 Slap, 26 Adopts,
27 Cheshire, 28 Lose one's, 29 Thread.
DOWN
1 Mass, 2 Hitchhike, 3 Dwarf, 4 Police, 5 Andre, 6
Operate, 7 Substitute, 12 Vault,
13 Off the wall, 15 Hetty, 17 Godfather, 19 Impious,
21 Crocus, 23 Outdo, 24 Sheet, 25 Mend.

QUIZ NO.2

Page 159
1. Germany, Italy, and Japan. 2. Fear of dogs.
3. Pierre Omidyar. 4. Prunes. 5. Snow White and
the Seven Dwarfs. 6. John Lennon. 7. Russia.
8. Sperm Whale. 9. Australia. 10. Rabbit. 11. A full
stop or exclamation point. 12. Ferdinand Magellan.
13. China. 14. Woodstock. 15. Three.

QUICK CROSSWORD NO.3

Page 166
ACROSS
1 Summit, 4 Sergeant, 8 In a state, 9 Hudson,
10 Prop, 11 Patience, 14 Rambler, 16 Collect, 18
Saveloy, 20 Sparrow, 22 Perisher, 24 Tome, 26
Trough, 27 Implying, 28 Hesitant, 29 Shrewd.
DOWN
1 Stir, 2 Miserable, 3 Tramp, 4 Sleepy, 5 Gaudí,
6 Absence, 7 Tinseltown, 12 Troop,
13 Crosspatch, 15 Enoch, 17 Lord mayor,
19 Various, 21 Artist, 23 Sight, 24 Tapas, 25 Aged.

QUIZ NO.3

Page 167
1. Twelve. 2. Marie Curie. 3. Tandoori. 4. Dorothy,
Rose, Blanche, and Sophia. 5. Nevada. 6. Coca
Cola. 7. Vatican City (It's less than two-tenths of
a square mile). 8. 'Henry's pockets' or cutaneous
marginal pouches. 9. Samsung. 10. Netherlands.
11. Canada. 12. Peter Pan. 13. Unkindness. 14. Spiny
Anteater, Long-Beaked Echidnas and the Duck-
Billed Platypus. 15. Robert Cawdrey.

QUICK CROSSWORD NO.4

Page 174
ACROSS
1 Sector, 4 Beef stew, 9 Pull-up, 10 Aversion, 12
Lion, 13 Joist, 14 Maze, 17 Evening dress,
20 Scene shifter, 23 Rome, 24 Adder, 25 Mass, 28
Starling, 29 Single, 30 Abridged, 31 Carrot.
DOWN
1 Supplier, 2 Calzones, 3 Opus, 5 Elvis Presley, 6
Fare, 7 Tribal, 8 Wanted, 11 Song and dance,
15 Pinch, 16 Aspic, 18 Stranger, 19 Prospect, 21
Cresta, 22 Impair, 26 Clod, 27 Visa.

QUIZ NO.4

Page 175
1. Four (Kenya, Uganda, Tanzania, and Somalia). 2.
Pacific Ocean. 3. Gin. 4. Candle in the Wind (1997).
5. 1989. 6. Arthur Conan Doyle. 7. Slovenia. 8. 22
months. 9. Qamar. 10. Star Trek. 11. Cuba.
12. Venus, with a temperature of 460 °C.
13. William Shakespeare. 14. Eight. 15. Tendons.